GRAIN POWER

PATRICIA GREEN
CAROLYN HEMMING

PINTAIL

ALSO BY PATRICIA GREEN & CAROLYN HEMMING

Quinoa Revolution
Quinoa 365

CONTENTS

PREFACE

*"Modern civilization has sacrificed much
of the quality of its food in the interests of
quantity and shelf life."*
—Michael Pollan, In Defense of Food

Why ancient grains? Because they haven't been messed with. They're simply ancient. Relatively untouched by modern methods, ancient grains take us back to our humble beginnings. We're quickly learning that the industrialization of food in the modern world has taken a toll on our health, and ancient grains can help to get us back on track. Whole and nutritious, ancient grains are purely good food that can help us to be well-nourished and healthy—and to survive.

North Americans and much of the modern world are in the midst of a transformation that is slowly changing where we buy our food, how we prepare our meals and what we put into our mouths—how we eat. Now, more than ever before, we want to know the significance and origins of what we feed our families, especially our children. We are even beginning to question what we feed our pets. With everyone we love threatened by serious illness, we understand more and more that poor eating can result in any number of health concerns. We are also now learning that many of our existing eating habits have been manufactured by

the food industry. We are increasing our awareness by asking more questions, demanding quality food and consuming less highly processed foods. Factory-prepared, boxed, brand slapped and heavily marketed convenience foods are becoming much less popular.

A closer relationship with food has reminded us of the comfort, wellness and pleasure we get from putting care and love into quality meals. Increasing health, social and environmental awareness has us paying more attention to whole, unprocessed foods, buying organic, finding out about the benefits of superfoods and seeking non-genetically-modified foods. Vegetarianism and gluten-free lifestyles are increasing at exponential rates. This food transformation has us wanting and appreciating the goodness of whole, pure, real, un-messed-with food—for the love of our families, of our health and of food.

Ancient grains. Organic, unprocessed, not genetically modified, vegan, superfood nutrition. Even without the confirmation of modern-day science, our ancient ancestors revered many of these seeds and grains and knew with absolute certainty that they could provide the proper nutrition to ensure their societies would be nourished, healthy and thriving. Only a few generations ago, when pioneering ancestors stopped to take a break on the farm and eat a cookie, it was likely healthy! If we bring back and incorporate ancient grains into what we are eating today, we can improve our nutrition, support optimal health and help to fight off disease and illness.

Since Patricia and I have been eagerly spreading the word about quinoa, we've been exploring the diversity and complexity of other ancient grains along the way. Already whole and genetically perfect, ancient grains are unmodified and worthy ingredients to explore for many reasons. Great taste, different textures, ideal nutrition and a variety of unique methods of preparation help to make ancient grains easy to incorporate into our modern-day menus. After all, eating the same

old thing doesn't do our health any good, but it also impacts us on a larger, global scale. Consuming foods (especially grains) that are biologically diverse is important. If we only eat corn and wheat, for instance (even beyond being completely bored), we end up contributing to a demand that promotes only a limited number of foods in the marketplace. By doing that, we are indirectly restricting the makeup of our food supply, which is obviously very dangerous.

So for whatever reason you are transforming your eating, we welcome you. We can assure you that the advantages of eating ancient grains are plenty. In our simple, uncomplicated recipe style, we hope to bring even more health, nutrition, enjoyment, fun, great taste and inspiration to your cooking experiences. We are pleased to be part of your personal food transformation and always encourage you to share your stories and feedback with us at **www.patriciaandcarolyn.com**.

Carolyn

Patricia

INTRODUCTION

WHAT ARE ANCIENT GRAINS?

Ancient grains have been around for centuries and provided important food sources for many ancient civilizations. Mysteriously, however, many ancient grains had been pretty much unheard of until they were recently rediscovered. Now generating new excitement, ancient grains are the answer to increasing our nutritional sources, and they're easy to cook at home. Sometimes referred to as "heritage grains," ancient grains are a superb alternative to the more common starchy and heavily processed foods North Americans have become used to eating.

Often included in the ancient grains category are amaranth, barley, buckwheat, einkorn, emmer, chia, farro, flax, Kamut, kañiwa, millet, oats, quinoa, rye, sorghum, spelt, spring wheat, teff, triticale, winter wheat and wild rice. Corn, wheat and rice also have ancient origins; in many cases, however, these foods have limited nutrition because they've been modified far beyond their ancient state.

Not all grains?

Although called ancient "grains" for culinary reasons, many are not even related to grains but have been grouped with them because of their cooking profile and similar nutrient content. Many of them are in fact seeds. Sometimes called pseudograins or pseudocereals, they may look like grains but are in fact fruit seeds that do not contain the gluten commonly found in many cereal grains. Coming

from broadleaf plants, these seeds can be used in much the same way as cereal grains and can also be cooked or ground into flour. Amaranth, buckwheat, chia, kañiwa, millet and quinoa are examples of gluten-free seeds or pseudograins. Traditional grains (cereal grains) are grasses and their starchy seeds are used as food. Some contain gluten and some do not. Examples of cereal grains are barley, farro, oats, sorghum, spelt, rye and teff. Specifically, oats, sorghum and teff are gluten-free cereal grains.

WHY USE ANCIENT GRAINS?

Ancient grains have a lot to offer and their appeal has made them fairly accessible to everyone— their availability is no longer restricted to health food stores or gourmet restaurants. Healthfulness and superfood properties are huge benefits, and ancient grains also provide unique textures and flavors that add a whole new dimension to many meals that you're already eating. The ease of cooking and versatility of ancient grains means you can easily incorporate them into your existing meals.

Along with great taste and added texture, the numerous advantages of adding ancient grains to your diet include adding fiber, complex carbohydrates (with a low glycemic impact, which means it won't spike your blood sugar), vitamins, minerals and disease-fighting antioxidants. So not only will your digestion be thanking you, but your body

Black quinoa

will be better armed to prevent diseases, maintain or lose weight, increase athletic performance and manage or prevent diabetes. As many of our families and friends are faced with serious illnesses, we are all slowly beginning to understand that what we are eating has an impact on our health. This awareness is the beginning of a societal shift in the right direction. Vegetarianism is one example of our ever-increasing eating awareness. Vegetarian lifestyles continue to rise exponentially as many consumers seek whole, organic and unmodified foods, superfoods and protein that is not from an animal source.

Either because of diabetes or to simply eat better, many people are now replacing or reducing their nutrient-inferior foods such as pasta and rice dishes. Ancient grains have the benefit of being a lower glycemic food that helps stabilize blood sugars and prevent insulin levels from spiking, which is thought to cause fat storage and, ultimately, weight gain. Increases in dietary disorders and food allergies have meant that the demand for gluten-free foods also continues to rise. Even people without diagnosed gluten intolerances are opting for a gluten-free lifestyle to improve their overall health. Gluten is known to initiate an inflammation response in the intestines that provokes a chain reaction with many other physiological processes—among other things, it can inhibit proper digestion and absorption of nutrients, weaken the immune response and cause allergies. The growing exodus of people moving away from gluten is also helping to push ancient grains back into the spotlight.

Eating ancient grains supports biodiversity! Choosing ancient grains encourages biodiversity by providing a demand for alternatives to traditional grains. When consumers choose the same grains all the time, it limits the demand for crop varieties, and farmers tend to grow what is most in demand. Less crop rotation and growing only genetically perfected grains results in a constant pursuit of disease-free plants that produce high yields and ignores the importance of biodiversity, nutrition and, critically, the future of our food supply. With up to 40 animal species relying on a crop, the threat of plant extinction is serious. To break it down, if 80,000 edible plant species exist but growers only concentrate on 150, then 90% of the traditional North American diet is made up of maybe 20 species. Scientists caution that if disease strikes a particular species we are dependent on, it can lead to serious consequences, even famine. So choosing a wider variety of grains is not only good for ensuring our own personal health, but it can help to ensure the continued existence of plants, all their interdependent species and our food supply.

Ancient grains tend to require less attention than modern grains and are therefore ideal subjects for organic farming. Modern crops, sensitive to the threat of disease and drought, require more pesticides and fertilizer. An ancient grain crop, organically farmed and rotated, helps give nutrition back to the land and does not threaten the environment. Modern-day methods of processing the most common grains we've been eating can also degrade nutrition. A huge benefit of ancient grains is that they are minimally processed, and in many cases they are simply winnowed, or cleanly removed from the plant, and then washed. Minimal processing means they can provide the maximum valuable minerals and vitamins that our bodies require.

As an alternative to overprocessed grains, ancient grains can increase the options for flavor and texture in a variety of recipes, including baking. Today, what we call "baking" is full of refined flours and heavily processed ingredients, and many would not consider baked goods healthful at all. Some would argue that baking, in general, was healthy when it was done with ancient grains. Milled in a more direct, simple manner, ancient grain flours can be more rustic and coarse, adding a pleasant texture that is out of the ordinary, has more flavor and fiber and is overall more wholesome and enjoyable.

It is becoming trendy to create recipes that venture beyond everyday ingredients and incorporate ancient grains. Using these grains is not overly expensive when you compare them to other organic products, healthy foods or traditional proteins—and most people aren't prepared to compromise the quality and nutrition of foods, especially when it means eating properly, avoiding allergies, defending against disease and providing overall nourishment for your family.

WHERE DO YOU FIND ANCIENT GRAINS?

Ancient grains were used and cultivated by many ancient civilizations and originate from a variety of locations, including Central and South America, Asia, Africa and Europe. Many of them still grow best in these areas and come from the same places to this day. Although maybe less familiar to us than rice or couscous, most ancient grains are readily available and not difficult to find. Commonly found at health food stores, a lineup of ancient grains can now also be found at popular bulk food stores and in special sections of your local grocery store in whole, flake, puff and flour formats. For those who live in isolated locations, most grains can be easily found online at sites that offer reasonable shipping rates.

WHAT SHOULD YOU LOOK FOR?

Whole grains are regarded as healthier than processed grains because the outside layer, containing higher amounts of fiber and additional nutrients, remains intact. Whole grains are generally cereal grains containing three main parts: the germ, bran and endosperm. Even if the outermost husk is removed (hulled), the original kernel should remain intact for the grain to be called a whole grain. Teff is such a small cereal grain that it cannot be hulled, so it definitely contains whole-grain nutrition. Although not true grains but seeds, we can include gluten-free pseudograins (also known as pseudocereals) such as amaranth, chia, buckwheat, kañiwa, millet, quinoa and sorghum in the category of whole grains because in most cases we consume the three parts—germ, bran and endosperm—together.

Which grains or seeds should be hulled?

The tough outermost layer of cellulose that covers a grain is the hull. Relatively indigestible, this layer may be high in fiber, but it does not contain much additional nutrition and in some cases prevents proper absorption of nutrients if it's not removed or opened (cracked). Most grains and seeds are best eaten hulled; otherwise, they can have an unpleasant taste and texture or may take a very long time to cook. Remember, even without the outermost hull, they are still considered *whole* grains. Most types of whole grains can be referred to as "groats," which really just means that the

grain has been washed and hulled (basic processing) and the inside kernel of the grain remains whole and intact.

Ground, cooked or raw?

In some cases, if a seed or grain you are eating still has the outermost shell completely intact, your body may not benefit from the seed's nutrition. The outer shell should at least be cracked, either by gentle cooking or pressure, such as grinding or hammering. Unground flax seeds, for instance, will pass right through the body without their nutrition being absorbed. Understanding when to open or crack the hull can be especially important for raw food eaters. As we've mentioned, teff is different and can be used by the body with the outer hull intact. The same also goes for chia. The outer shells of chia break down in the body easily, so they don't need to be ground to be digested and their nutrients absorbed.

Some of those who cook with grains consider it valuable to soak them prior to cooking. This is simply done by soaking them in water in a warm environment or with an enzyme-rich ingredient such as kefir, yogurt or whey (this latter process is also known as fermenting). In some cases, for instance with sorghum grains, a certain amount of processing or breaking down of the grains is important in improving the overall nutritive value. Some believe that soaking all grains can help to further improve digestion and mineral absorption. If this is your preference, you will find that you may need to adjust cooking times.

GMO or certified organic?

Many people are concerned about the largely unknown effects of consuming genetically modified (GM) or genetically engineered (GE) food products that are in the market today. One benefit to choosing ancient grains is that they are not currently tampered with by genetic modification. Most ancient grains are already naturally genetically complex and have become inherently strong crops from surviving thousands of years of harsh growing conditions in their natural environments. However, we recommend using products that specify on the label that they are NOT genetically modified. This will become increasingly important as large, crop-dominating companies genetically alter and develop seeds in their fierce attempt to breed crops that will grow well in areas outside of their natural environments to cash in on the profits. At the very least, we recommend that you use only those grains and seeds certified organic. Note that there is some debate about "organic" labeling being inadequate for genetically modified products, so you may want to be absolutely sure by purchasing only products specifically labeled as not genetically modified.

Support fair trade!

The increasing global demand for some ancient grains means it is important to be aware of buying fair trade. Buying products certified as fair trade assures that the ancient grains are grown in healthy, sustainable environments where farmers and their land are not exploited. If we want ancient grains to enrich our lives, we should also be vigilant to ensure that growing families are fairly and positively supported as well.

What about storage?

All seeds, grains and flours should be kept out of direct sunlight and in a cool, dry place. Most

Red quinoa

of them will deteriorate quickly in warmer, more humid climates, so refrigerate them if necessary. Whole seeds generally last the longest, some even for many years if stored correctly. Flour lasts the shortest time, as it has been ground; however, it can remain fresh for months if stored properly. We recommend that you grind seeds only as necessary or buy smaller amounts of flour to ensure you've always got the freshest supply on hand.

As your stock of ancient grains begins to fill the cupboards, the need to organize them will become increasingly important. Many of these grains can look very similar, so proper labeling is key. You will want to be able to distinguish between the different types of seeds, grains and flours when you're in a hurry and ready to cook. Be as practical or creative as you would like! All kinds of fun and interesting storage containers and labels can be bought at office supply or craft stores and even online. We have two favorite ideas we think are the most efficient and cost-effective solutions to organize all your favorite new pantry additions. Use one or both ways to keep things tidy!

- If you're just starting out and still trying to find out what works best for you, *or* you have a small storage area *or* just need a place to keep smaller amounts of ingredients organized, a large clear sealable tote with labeled freezer bags may work best.

  Keep this tote in your pantry or bottom cupboard for quick and easy access.
- If you have ample cupboard space, the best way to organize multiple ancient grains and keep them dry and fresh is with sealed clear glass mason jars. Glass is non-reactive and provides a good storage solution, especially if you have multiple grains in larger amounts. Various sizes are available, contents are easy to see, and labels can be on the lid as well as the side of the jar for quick and easy access.

A number of label options are available, and many of them are sure to dress up your cupboard space and make you look like an ancient grains pro! We like black chalkboard-style labels and writing on them with white chalk or grease pencils, or printable vintage labels and tags. For refrigerator or freezer items such as ground flours, we recommend either mason jars (refrigerator only) or labeled sealable plastic bags (freezer).

HOW TO USE THIS BOOK

We encourage you to experiment with as many ancient grains as your dietary requirements allow. This book exclusively uses ancient grains and seeds that are *gluten-free*, including amaranth, buckwheat, chia, kañiwa, millet, oats, quinoa, sorghum and teff. These gluten-free ancient grains produced the best results for us, providing the most flavor, versatility and applications. The first chapter will provide you with everything you need to know about preparing each specific ancient grain. You will also find that most of the recipes list more than one ancient grain. This is because a combination of ancient grains may often provide the best texture, flavor, nutrition or overall appearance.

Incorporating a variety of ancient grains into your meals is the best strategy for a healthy lifestyle. In the case of flour, blends are usually required to provide a combination of necessary characteristics to create a proper texture, taste and density and ensure that your hard work in the kitchen results in a successful final product. We have included substitutes for many of the seeds and flours, and these will allow you to be creative and tailor the recipes to your specific needs and preferences.

Gluten-free?

All the recipes in this book are made with seeds and grains that are gluten-free; however, if you are sensitive to or deliberately avoiding gluten, ensure that you purchase products that are processed in gluten-free facilities and are clearly labeled as such on the package. In the past, some products have caused confusion when inadequate labeling has caused people to believe a product actually contains gluten when in fact it has just been contaminated with wheat products or other sources of gluten. Obviously, for some, this is just as dangerous, but it is an important distinction nonetheless. All the recipes in this book can be made gluten-free. If you must ensure that recipes are completely gluten-free, always make sure that the ingredients you use are consistently labeled as such. Each region will have different products available—such as Worcestershire sauce, tamari, oats, buns, sour cream and more—that meet gluten free standards.

Using alternatives

Any alternatives for preparing a recipe, including our recommendations for substituting other ancient grains, are clearly stated in each recipe. A recipe may read *buckwheat* in the ingredients list, for example, but also indicate that you may use *millet* or *quinoa* in the same recipe. These alternatives allow you to choose varying possibilities for preparation, depending on your personal palate,

specific nutritional requirements or what you may have in your cupboard.

Are there standard instructions for grains?

Many times, people have asked us if there are standard instructions for preparing all grains or seeds, flours or flakes. We wish cooking was that straightforward! However, different recipes and each grain's unique characteristics mean that every recipe has instructions that depend on a variety of conditions. For best results, we recommend carefully following each recipe. However, we also want you to be inspired to be creative and experiment yourself!

In Chapter 1, instructions for basic preparation of each ancient grain are provided, along with a nutritional profile, unique cooking properties, specific flavor affinities, tips for storage and any additional instructions for sprouting, toasting or using in raw food.

Thickeners and stabilizers

Where some recipes require a thickener or stabilizer, we use xanthan gum. This is especially valuable in recipes that do not contain gluten. A natural carbohydrate, xanthan gum can replace gluten and helps to bind and add volume to gluten-free baking. Guar gum is also a popular stabilizer and behaves very similarly to xanthan gum. Xanthan gum originates from corn and guar gum from legumes. Overuse of either can make your baked goods too heavy. Guar gum is a good alternative if you have corn allergies, but it is very high in fiber and can cause stomach upset, especially if you are sensitive or it is not used sparingly. The general rule is to add approximately 1 tsp (5 mL) for every 1 cup

(250 mL) of gluten-free flour in recipes that rise a lot, and ½ tsp (2 mL) for recipes that don't require as much leavening. In our recipes, we have consistently used xanthan gum if a binding agent is required. You may use guar gum if you prefer, but results may differ slightly.

Using oil in recipes

Deciding which oil to use in a recipe can be confusing. Oil can be a healthier alternative to butter, since it contains more unsaturated, rather than saturated, fats. But how do you choose the healthiest oil that will also taste great?

Overall, vegetable oils used for cooking are generally healthy because they originate from plants. The healthiest of oils contain the most monounsaturated fats, are less refined and are higher in nutrients. These include virgin olive oil and peanut, canola, flaxseed, walnut, hemp, avocado and almond oils. Labels saying "extra virgin" or "unrefined" mean the oil is less processed and therefore contains even more nutrients.

An important factor in ensuring that you are using cooking oils in a healthy manner depends on whether the recipe requires cooking. High temperatures will cause the nutritional profile of oils to break down and change, becoming less healthy, so it is important to choose the appropriate oil for each application.

Oils that have a higher smoke point (point at which they burn) are the best for cooking at high temperatures. Grapeseed, vegetable, canola, corn, sunflower, safflower, peanut or a refined olive oil have a higher smoke point and are better for cooked recipes such as granolas, pilafs, waffles and frittatas. Recipes that do not require cooking, such as salads and dips, can use oils that are more pure and less refined. These include extra virgin olive oil and flaxseed, walnut and hemp oil.

A note on nutritional values

Nutritional values in this book are always based on the first option provided in the recipe. For instance, if the ingredient option is "vegetable or chicken stock," the nutritional values provided are based on vegetable stock. Also, optional ingredients are not included in the nutritional values.

OVERVIEW OF ANCIENT GRAINS
Amaranth

Amaranthus, from the spinach family, is a small seed about the size of a sesame seed and light brown or golden in color. It is a pseudograin with characteristics similar to traditional grains, but in reality it is a seed. Amaranth contains plenty of complex carbohydrates and it is completely gluten-free. Even though ancient grains have been around for a long time, some research remains to be done, so there is much conflicting information on the levels of amino acids in amaranth and whether or not it is a complete protein. Although amaranth does appear to contain all the essential amino acids, it does not seem to have sufficient levels of two of them (threonine and leucine), therefore making it incomplete.

Both amaranth leaves and seeds can be consumed, though the seeds are most commonly eaten and can be made into flour and flakes. You can also find puffed amaranth, or make it yourself, similar to popping corn. Amaranth is not currently genetically modified and is a pure and natural, whole, ancient food.

Originating in Central and South America, amaranth is said to be between 6,000 and 8,000 years

Millet puffs

Quinoa flakes

old. The ancient Aztecs worshipped, consumed and incorporated amaranth into their religious practices for its supernatural powers. The attempts by the Spanish to convert the Aztecs to Christianity meant that foods associated with any of their religious practices were to be destroyed and anyone discovered possessing the seeds faced severe punishment. Thankfully, amaranth was secretly cultivated by a few brave individuals in remote areas of Mexico and the Andes; otherwise, it would most certainly be extinct today. Amaranth's hardiness and ability to grow quickly also helped to secure its existence and its return to North American plates around the 1970s.

Today, amaranth is largely grown in Mexico, Peru, Nepal and Bolivia and smaller amounts are also grown in the United States, Africa, China, India and Russia.

As a crop, amaranth is relatively easy to cultivate. It grows very quickly, and despite the small size of the seeds, they are easily harvested with traditional grain equipment. With more than 60 species in the family, amaranth is a plant that survives a variety of conditions and soil types, although it prefers higher elevations and well-drained soil. Adaptable to many different climates, it can even thrive in very dry climates once the seed has been established.

Buckwheat

Although the word "wheat" is in the name, buckwheat is related to rhubarb and not to the wheat family at all. In fact, *Fagopyrum esculentum* is a seed and considered a pseudograin or pseudocereal. Buckwheat seeds are brown and pyramid-shaped. Kernels are called kasha once they have been roasted. Gluten-free and high in complex carbohydrates, buckwheat also contains all the essential amino acids to make it a complete protein. It is not currently genetically modified and the seeds can be purchased as kasha (roasted), as groats (unroasted, light brown or green inner seeds, flakes or puffs) and as flour, found in dark or light variations.

Buckwheat is approximately 8,000 years old and is thought to have originated in Siberia, high in the Himalayan mountains and in Manchuria. It was a favorite of Buddhist monks, who helped spread it to other Asian countries. Traders then brought buckwheat from Asia to Europe, where it has remained a popular food in Central Europe and Russia. Now it is primarily grown in China, Australia and Canada, where it grows quickly and is resilient even in inferior soil conditions and cooler climates. The sweet nectar of buckwheat flowers attracts bees, and buckwheat honey is often the delicious result.

Chia

Another gluten-free pseudograin, chia, or *Salvia hispanica,* is actually a species of the mint family and related to sage. Considered an oil seed, it is not an actual grain but has tremendous nutritional value as a seed nonetheless. Chia seeds can be white, brown or black in color (often with spotted, uneven red or brown patches) and small and oval in shape.

Chia is considered a complete protein, so it can be eaten without adding any other ingredients, making it easy for the body to digest and benefit from the seed's wide range of powerful nutrients. Chia is acclaimed for many favorable properties, including a high content of antioxidants, complex carbohydrates, fiber, omega-3 and omega-6 fatty

Chewy Chocolate Granola
with Cherries & Buckwheat

acids and protein (for more on chia nutrition, see page 14). Chia can be bought in whole-seed or ground forms.

Like many nutritious grains and seeds, it is also sold as a healthy additive for animal feed, especially to enhance foods produced for human consumption, including, eggs, chicken and milk. Chia sold for human consumption in North America is not currently genetically modified.

Over 5,000 years old, chia was another grain cultivated and revered by the ancient Aztecs, Maya and Southwest Native American tribes. Valued so highly it was sometimes used as currency, it was eaten, like a few other ancient grains, as a source of energy, especially during times of war. Seeds were roasted, ground and mixed with water to make a gel that was consumed in small amounts.

Chia seeds grow easily, as many may remember from sprouting them in the once popular Chia Pets. Chia seeds grow well in drier, hot climates such as Mexico, Central and South America, Australia and areas of western North America.

Kañiwa

Kañiwa, also known as cañahua and cañawa, is quickly increasing in popularity. It is related to quinoa and is often called baby quinoa because of its small size. Although indeed smaller than its quinoa cousin, *Chenopodium pallidicaule* is a pale gray to red seed that is a deep brownish red color when cooked. It has no saponin coating (which may cause a slightly bitter taste in quinoa) and has a milder and sweeter flavor. Slightly higher in protein and fiber than quinoa, kañiwa is another gluten-free superfood with a stellar nutritional profile including being a complete protein and containing complex carbohydrates. (For more

information on kañiwa's nutritional profile, see page 16). It can currently be purchased as whole seeds or flour. As with other ancient grains, it is not currently genetically modified because of its inherent, naturally complex genetic makeup.

Like quinoa, kañiwa originated in South America thousands of years ago and was a staple food of the Incan and Aztec cultures. Today it still grows in South America, primarily around Lake Titicaca on both the Bolivian and the Peruvian sides. Best grown in high altitudes, kañiwa is said to be tolerant of even tougher climate conditions than quinoa.

Millet

One of the oldest of the ancient grains, millet is often overlooked because of its reputation as food for the birds. Also known in India as *bajra*, millet sold for human consumption in North America is primarily pearl millet (*Pennisetum glaucum*). Although millet is not a traditional grain, it is a seed, or pseudograin, that is often grouped into the grain category because it behaves similarly to grains when cooked.

A small, round, pale seed, millet is a nutritious, gluten-free energy source that contains protein and plenty of complex carbohydrates. There remains some confusion about whether or not millet is a complete protein; however, it is lacking in the essential amino acid lysine and so cannot be considered a complete protein. (For more information on millet's nutritional properties, see page 18).

Believed to be around 10,000 years old, millet is likely to have originated in Africa and spread to Asia. Today it is grown beyond those continents and can be found in North America and Europe. Millet has definitely stood the test of time. Ideally, it grows quickly in fertile, well-drained soil, but like most resilient ancient grains, it is hardy and may also thrive in soil that is dry, acidic and of poor fertility.

At the time of writing this book, millet is grown from traditional seeds and is not genetically modified. It can be found in a variety of forms including flour, puffs and flakes.

Oats

The oat, *Avena sativa,* is an ancient grain that truly can be called a grain. Over 4,000 years old, oats have been a highly popular cereal grain (grass) for generations. It is a whole grain that most of us have eaten at some point in our lives, perhaps because oats are one of the cheapest of the ancient grains.

Three of the most common forms are rolled (old-fashioned, large flake), quick-cooking (or instant) and steel-cut. Rolled and quick-cooking oats have been flattened, steamed and toasted, whereas steel-cut oats are whole oats that have simply been chopped up into chunks. (Nutritional differences do exist; see page 19.) A version of "quick" steel-cut oats also exists.

Oats are packed with nutrition, mainly complex carbohydrates and protein, but are not a complete protein. Currently not genetically modified, this ancient grain can be a valuable asset in gluten-free cooking.

Originating as a secondary crop (meaning it was first a weed among other crops, such as wheat), it was later cultivated as a crop on its own. The number of species make it difficult to trace exactly where oats come from, but it is thought to have originated in Swiss caves or from Asia Minor (Turkey). It is a popular crop in Scotland and Ireland, where the climate is cooler and rainfall is plentiful. The early 1600s marks the first oat crops grown in moderate climates of North America, where, in addition to Europe, it is now primarily grown.

Quinoa

A popular favorite in the past few years, quinoa is a superfood that satisfies many cooking styles and applications. *Chenopodium quinoa* is a pseudo-grain and truly a fruit or seed from a broadleaf plant related to spinach. This little white (golden), red or black seed has a distinctive little tail that uncurls from the seed when cooked. Known for being gluten-free and a complete protein containing complex carbohydrates and a realm of vitamins and minerals, quinoa boasts a nutritional profile that puts many other whole foods to shame.

Found in seed, flake, puff or flour formats, this versatile ancient grain can be prepared in a wide variety of impressive recipes that fulfill today's spectrum of vegan, gluten-free and traditional North American meal requirements.

Quinoa was one of the foods worshipped by ancient Incas, who weaned their babies on quinoa and thought it gave their people special strength. Spanish conquistadors, threatened by quinoa's "power," intended to destroy every last quinoa seed, believing it the food of the devil. Thankfully, it was so cherished by Incans that some even risked their lives to hide seeds and grow quinoa in hidden patches high up in the mountains of South America, ensuring it would be around for many generations to come.

Genetic complexity is a natural characteristic of quinoa, and the seed doesn't need to be genetically engineered, as it has developed the ability to survive tough soil and weather conditions. It is

for these reasons that this ancient grain of 5,000-plus years is still around to this day. It grows best in relatively dry, well-drained soil and can tolerate high altitudes. It is not currently genetically modified. Quinoa is grown primarily in Bolivia, Ecuador, Peru and other areas of South America and also in Europe, the United States and Canada.

Sorghum

Accurately called a grain, *Sorghum bicolor* is a true cereal grass referred to as milo, Johnson grass or *jowar* in India. Red and white varieties of this gluten-free, complex carbohydrate–rich seed are sold in grain or flour form. Sorghum contains protein but is an incomplete protein because of low levels of the essential amino acid lysine.

Over 5,000 years old, sorghum originated in Africa but has been grown in the United States since the 1950s, particularly for use in the making of sweeteners from the plant's stalk, or cane. Sorghum syrup and hot biscuits are a popular breakfast in the southern United States.

Sorghum is affordable and a popular ingredient in gluten-free cooking and baking. Some sorghum may be genetically modified, so ensure that you buy organic product that specifies it is not genetically modified. In the past, modified sorghum

seeds have been introduced in Africa, especially engineered to resist aluminum contamination and meet the needs specific to this region and environment. Africa, Central America and South Asia are the main sorghum growers, where hot, dry climates and low to no humidity are ideal for its finely branched root system.

Teff

The smallest of the ancient grains, *Eragrostis tef* is another true cereal grain. Although mostly found in a dark brown color, some lighter varieties can also be found. Over 5,000 years old, teff is also known as love grass, thaff or thaft. It is a gluten-free, complete protein that is high in complex carbohydrates and is an essential product of the food supply, especially in Ethiopia. For years, teff has been harvested and ground into flour to make *injera*, a popular, spongy African flatbread.

Also grown in the United States, teff is not currently genetically modified and has a range of growing capabilities that allow it to withstand high heat and infertile, dry soil or even the extreme opposite, flooded areas. Teff is an efficient crop to grow, and in only three short months a single pound of grain can produce an entire acre of crop.

Chocolate Ancient Grain Torte
with Raspberry Chia Sauce

EASY
ANCIENT GRAIN
BASICS

Whether you're just beginning to incorporate ancient grains into your lifestyle or you've been cooking with them for some time, this chapter will provide a quick reference to everything you need to have at your fingertips—from descriptions of flavor and texture, basic cooking techniques, unique cooking properties, nutritional breakdowns, available forms (such as flakes, flour or seeds), storage, use as a raw food, sprouting or toasting instructions and helpful buying information. We will even tell you how to make your own flours and dairy-free milk using gluten-free ancient grains—everything to ensure that you become a true expert!

Making Your Own Flour

Generally, all seeds and grains (whole or flaked) can be made into flour. And flour is always the healthiest if it is made from the whole seed, which contains the most nutritional integrity. While store-bought milled flour is a finer grind, milling your own can be an economical and healthier way of incorporating ancient grains into your diet.

For smaller amounts, grinding can be done using a simple mortar and pestle. For larger amounts, a coffee grinder, seed mill or a good blender can be used. Caution when using flour grinders! Depending on the grinder, the oil in some seeds or grains can ruin an expensive model. Also keep in mind that grind results can differ, depending on the appliance used. A high-end blender or coffee grinder should result in a grind that is similar to a "meal" and may feel coarse when rubbed between your fingers. It is important to note that this type of flour may make for heavier density in baking recipes.

To make flour, first place a small amount of seeds, grains or flakes in your appliance. When you are familiar with how much your appliance can handle, adjust the amount that you grind per batch to produce the desired flour consistency. If you wish, sift the flour to remove any larger pieces. Larger remaining pieces can be ground repeatedly. Continue processing your flour until you have the desired amount. Store in a sealed container in the refrigerator or freezer to extend shelf life.

Toasting Grains and Seeds

OVEN METHOD: Preheat the oven to 350°F (180°C). Place the seeds or flour on a baking sheet and bake for 5 to 7 minutes, until fragrant and you smell a "toasted" aroma.

STOVETOP METHOD: Place the seeds, grains or flour in a large dry saucepan on medium heat. Stir for 3 to 5 minutes, until fragrant and you smell a "toasted" aroma.

In both toasting methods, watch closely, as seeds, grains and flour can all burn very quickly. Toasted seeds, grains and flour may not change color too much, even when completely toasted. They can add a new dimension of flavor to your recipes.

Puffed and Popped Grains

You can purchase puffed buckwheat, quinoa, amaranth, sorghum and millet in stores or online. Purchasing is the best option if you want to use the puffs for cereals or snack bars. Puffs are tender, while popped grains have more crunch. If you want to pop your own seeds, amaranth and sorghum are the easiest. Teff and quinoa will pop, but we've found the final result is inconsistent and may seem hardly worth the effort. See instructions for making popped amaranth on page 11 and popped sorghum on page 26.

Superblends

Superblend recipes provide alternatives to using a single ancient grain or seed in a recipe. Superblends incorporate nutrition from multiple ancient grains and can be used in almost any recipe where a single whole ancient grain is used. Superblends also provide an option for those who are not accustomed to the flavor of a particular grain. Combining multiple grains also helps neutralize the overall flavor and allows for more cooking versatility.

Recipes in this book will indicate where superblends provide the best results. See tables below.

We find both of the following blends provide the best flavor, texture and cooking combinations. Integrate these superblends into your own favorite recipes or, depending on your taste preferences, experiment and create your own superblends.

In a medium saucepan, stir together the ingredients for the blend you have chosen. Bring to a boil, then reduce to a simmer. Cover and cook, 20 minutes for Superblend 1 and 15 minutes for Superblend 2. Remove from the heat. Fluff with a fork and use as desired.

Making Your Own Dairy-Free Milk from Seeds and Grains

These days, you can buy almost any nut, soy or grain milk from grocery stores. But why not make your own wholesome, homemade and dairy-free milk with your favorite grains or seeds? Use purchased flour or flakes to make milk, or increase the nutrition even further by using fresh whole seeds or grains. Milks last up to 5 days in the

SUPERBLEND 1—QUINOA, MILLET, BUCKWHEAT/KAÑIWA, AMARANTH/TEFF

YIELD (cooked)	QUINOA (uncooked)	MILLET (uncooked)	BUCKWHEAT GROATS OR KAÑIWA (uncooked)	AMARANTH OR TEFF (uncooked)	WATER
1¾ cups (325 mL)	¼ cup (60 mL)	2 Tbsp (30 mL)	1 Tbsp + 1½ tsp (22 mL)	1½ tsp (7 mL)	1 cup (250 mL)
3 cups (750 mL)	½ cup (125 mL)	¼ cup (60 mL)	3 Tbsp (45 mL)	1 Tbsp (15 mL)	2 cups (500 mL)

SUPERBLEND 2—QUINOA, BUCKWHEAT/MILLET

YIELD (cooked)	QUINOA (uncooked)	BUCKWHEAT GROATS OR MILLET (hulled, uncooked)	WATER
1½ cups (325 mL)	¼ cup (60 mL)	¼ cup (60 mL)	1 cup (250 mL)
3 cups (750 mL)	½ cup (125 mL)	½ cup (125 mL)	2 cups (500 mL)

GRAIN	SOAKING TIME	SPROUT LENGTH	SPROUTING TIME	YIELD
Amaranth	24 hours, rinsing every 8 to 10 hours	⅛ to ¼ inch (3 to 5 mm) or when live (green)	3 to 4 days	½ cup (125 mL) = ½ to ⅔ cup (125 to 150 mL)
Kañiwa	24 hours, rinsing every 8 to 10 hours	⅛ inch (3 mm) or when live (green)	3 to 4 days	½ cup (125 mL) = ½ to ⅔ cup (125 to 150 mL)
Quinoa	1 to 4 hours	⅛ to ½ inch (3 mm to 1 cm)	1 to 3 days	½ cup (125 mL) = 1 cup (250 mL)
Teff	1 to 4 hours	⅛ to ¼ inch (3 to 5 mm)	1 to 4 days	½ cup (125 mL) = ½ to ⅔ cup (125 to 150 mL)
Buckwheat groats, Millet, Oats,	Buy sprouting-grade seeds online or in specialty stores.		Follow directions on package.	

refrigerator. (For chia milk, keep in mind that the final result will be gelatinous.) The milk from quinoa, kañiwa, oat or millet can be made creamier by gently simmering for 4 minutes prior to straining (strain once).

Sprouting

Sprouting is a raw method of preparing your grains and seeds that can provide a living, nutrient-rich alternative to cooked foods. Most grains and seeds can be sprouted at home using a simple method. Amaranth, buckwheat, kañiwa, quinoa, millet and teff can all be sprouted using various methods, though specific sprouting-grade seeds may be needed for buckwheat and millet. Sorghum is not recommended for sprouting, as the seeds have been known to generate high levels of cyanide when soaked in liquids or sprouted.

Sprouts are a great way to grow your own fresh food any time of the year, and you can't get any more local than your own kitchen! It is also becoming increasingly popular to eat raw, sprouted foods, which are full of enzymes and rich in vitamins and minerals. Sprouts can be eaten as a nutritious

TIP: Save yourself time by securing cheesecloth over the opening of a mason jar, using the rim of the lid without the sealer top. Pour water directly into the jar and then rinse and pour out the water without having to transfer the contents to a strainer. Set mason jars on their sides and shake seeds so they are fairly even along the side of the jar. Purchase mason jar strainer covers or make your own with rust-resistant window screening that fits snugly under the rim of the sealer ring.

snack all on their own, used in cold recipes such as salads, or added to sandwiches.

For sprouts, use organic seeds and grains when possible, as they have been handled in a manner that reduces the risk of contamination. When sprouting, cleanliness is critical to ensure that there is no chance of contamination, which is possible during any kind of sprouting process. Quinoa and teff are the quickest-sprouting seeds. Sprouts

DAIRY-FREE SEED OR GRAIN MILK

½ cup (125 mL) whole amaranth, buckwheat
    groats, chia, kañiwa, millet, steel-cut oats,
    quinoa or teff seeds, flakes or flour
4 to 6 cups (1 to 1.5 L) cold water
2 tsp (10 mL) pure vanilla extract
Honey, pure maple syrup or favorite sweetener,
    to taste

Preheat a saucepan to medium heat. Place
the seeds, flakes or flour in the pan and whisk
frequently until lightly toasted and fragrant.
Remove from the heat and allow to cool
completely. If using seeds or flakes, place in
a coffee grinder, seed grinder or blender and
grind as fine as possible, as close as you can
to flour. Place toasted flour in a large bowl
or container with the cold water and stir.
Wait 10 minutes, until the flour settles. Stir
and allow the flour to settle again. Stir once
more and pour through a fine-mesh strainer
into a pitcher or glass jar. Stir in the vanilla
and desired sweetener and serve. Each time
you serve, shake or stir quickly. Keep in the
refrigerator for up to 5 days. Milk makes a
great drink on its own or serve it on cereal.

*Note: Sorghum is not recommended for
making milk.*

are best when eaten small because they have more
crunch and last longer. Sprouts that are larger
and longer are softer in texture and deteriorate
more quickly.

TO SPROUT SEEDS

Wash your hands thoroughly. Place the seeds
in a clean glass casserole dish (do not use
plastic; it can have residual bacteria that may
contaminate your sprouts). Pour in enough
distilled water to cover the seeds, stir with
a clean spoon and soak for required time at
room temperature for the first 4 hours and the
remainder in a cool place.

Drain the water from the seeds using a wire
strainer. While in the strainer, rinse the seeds
with more distilled water. Rinse the casserole
dish. Return the drained and wet seeds to the
casserole dish and replace the cover, leaving a
slight opening for air. Place in the refrigerator
or a dark, cool location. Repeat the rinsing
process every 8 to 10 hours until the seeds
have sprouted to desired length.

Store prepared sprouts in a glass container in
the refrigerator with the lid open slightly to allow
for air circulation. It is best to use sprouts within
1 to 3 days of achieving desired length. Do not
eat them if they have any odor, slime or visible
mold, which can sometimes result from lack of
air circulation, not enough rinsing or sprouting
in too warm an environment. The final quantity
of sprouts will depend on the time the sprouts
grow and their resulting length. Recipes that
feature sprouts include Strawberry & Mango Quinoa Sprout Smoothie (page 34) and Vietnamese
Vegetable Noodle Soup with Quinoa Sprouts
(page 120).

Rolled oat flakes

Ground chia seeds

Amaranth seeds

Kañiwa seeds

Buckwheat groats

Teff grains

Sorghum flour

Millet seeds

Red quinoa seeds

Microgreens

Other grains or seeds have certain characteristics that require them to be grown as microgreens. Microgreens are generally referred to as tiny young edible plants that are harvested for their nutrition and flavor. Often grown vertically, microgreens can be grown either in soil or on a felt pad or in some type of fabric (in contrast, sprouting is done with the seeds or grains soaking in a mass bunched together in a container) and are another great way to grow food in your own home regardless of where you live. They can be eaten in salads, sandwiches or smoothies, juiced, used as garnishes or even eaten alone. Some research suggests that eating these immature fresh microgreens has even more benefits than consuming them in their mature state, as young plants have been found to contain higher levels of nutrients.

Most seeds and grains can be sown as microgreens. As with sprouts, millet, buckwheat and oats should be purchased specifically as sprouting-grade seeds (online or via specialty stores). Follow instructions on the package. Some seeds are easier to grow than others. Chia, teff and quinoa, for example, germinate and grow quickly, so they are great to start with, while others may take a bit of practice. Whole chia seeds (like flax seeds) are often grown best as microgreens because they are mucilaginous, or have gel-like properties that make soaking them for sprouting tricky because it often results in a gel instead of sprouts. *Note:* Sorghum is not recommended for growing as microgreens.

We suggest starting with a smaller amount of seeds until you become familiar with how they grow, as this will help avoid any waste. When you feel you have enough know-how, plant a large tray or multiple containers of microgreens.

To begin, you will need either plastic food trays or containers with lids, or you can purchase sprouting trays from your local growing centre. With a little patience and practice, it is possible to plant microgreens in almost any container. In addition, you will need your choice of seed, a spray bottle, cheesecloth (optional), scissors or a knife and a piece of cardboard or newspaper to cover.

Microgreens can be grown inside or out, but to ensure the best possible product (no windblown dirt or feeding insects or local wildlife), we suggest indoors. To give the seeds the best possible start, soak the seeds prior to planting them. Although this is not necessary, it will save growing time. Soak quinoa, teff and chia for 12 hours before planting. Soak kañiwa and amaranth for 24 hours before planting. The following cheesecloth method will help you soak not only the regular seeds but also mucilaginous seeds such as chia.

CHEESECLOTH METHOD: Cut a piece of cheesecloth to fit inside the growing vessel, making sure that it has been doubled up twice so that you can place seeds in the middle like a sandwich with two layers of cheesecloth on each side of the seeds. Place the cloth on a rimmed baking sheet and open the cheesecloth into two halves. Sprinkle seeds sparingly (about ¼ inch/5 mm apart) and cover with the other half of the cloth. Gently pour water over the cheesecloth and seeds and let soak for the appropriate time. When it comes time to rinse, gently fold the cheesecloth into a manageable size and place in a wire mesh strainer. Rinse gently every 8 to 10 hours and allow to drain briefly. Gently unfold it back on the baking sheet and soak in water again. Rinse again, if necessary, drain and place into your growing vessel (ensure there are holes in the bottom for drainage and at least 1 inch/2.5 cm of moist organic potting soil in the bottom). Cover with lid, cardboard or newspaper with small openings for air circulation. Set out of direct sunlight to prevent premature drying of soil. Water by spraying with the water bottle until moist but not soaked (you may not have to do this the first time you lay your cheesecloth on the soil). The soil should always be moist to the touch but not soaking. You may have to spray with a water bottle twice a day, if necessary. Remove the cover and place in partial or full sun once the plants have grown to 1 inch (2.5 cm). Although covering is not necessary at this stage, it seems to maintain the soil moisture longer. The seedlings will be ready to harvest when they are about 2 to 3 inches (5 to 8 cm) high. If your seedlings get too large, their texture and flavor may become less palatable. Harvest microgreens by cutting with scissors or a knife just above the cheesecloth.

Start another planting of microgreens about 5 days after the first one. Once the entire vessel of microgreens has been used up, you will have to start over by removing old stems, reworking the soil and planting again.

There are a few things to keep in mind while you are waiting for your microgreens to grow. Seeds will not grow if they are overwatered, underwatered, have poor air circulation, are planted too close together, are infertile or are presoaked too little or too long. Overwatering and poor circulation may cause mold, like small spider webs, to appear on your microgreens.

Some seeds will take longer to get started, so be patient. If your seeds don't grow at all, start over with different seeds. It is always trial and error, and a variety of different methods can be found online. We encourage you to experiment with sprouting and growing your own microgreens with ancient grains!

COOKING ANCIENT GRAINS

There are many ways to cook ancient grains. In this chapter, we provide our best recommendations for cooking each seed or grain. These methods will provide you with what we consider the most preferable results for cooked ancient grains. You may find our recommended cooking processes much quicker than many existing methods.

Amaranth

FLAVOR: malty, herbaceous, woody, mild, nutty, sweet, earthy

TEXTURE: sticky, al dente, gelatinous

FORMS: whole seeds, flour, flakes, puffs, leaves (where available)

GLUTEN-FREE ✔

COMPLETE PROTEIN ✗

Cooking with Amaranth

Like many ancient grains, amaranth can take on the flavor of whatever it is cooked with. It can be used as a thickener and is often used to make roux, sauces and gravy. Amaranth also pops, much like popcorn but smaller.

The most commonly cooked amaranth recipes include breakfast cereals, muesli, stir-fries, cookies, breads, soups, doughs, ice cream and even candy. It is popular combined with beans and chicken and can be used in mole sauce. Because of its naturally sweet flavor, amaranth works well with recipes that have honey, maple syrup or brown sugar.

Amaranth flour is excellent for quick breads and is often used in flatbreads. The recommended

Amaranth seeds

amount of amaranth flour in baking is around 25%. Too much amaranth flour may cause baking to brown too quickly or even create a bitter flavor, depending on other flavors it is mixed with. As with many gluten-free flours, it can produce very dense baked goods if too much is used or it is used exclusively.

Amaranth seeds and flour can be toasted before cooking or baking. This releases and deepens the flavor, adding a mildly fragrant aroma (see toasting method on page 2).

Nutrition

Amaranth is a good source of magnesium, phosphorus, manganese, iron, folate and unsaturated fat and is exceptionally rich in calcium. Like most ancient grains, amaranth is a great source of dietary fiber. It is also high in protein, especially in the amino acid lysine, which is often deficient in other seeds and cereal grains. Although studies have confirmed that the quality of dietary protein is high, amaranth has lower levels of two essential amino acids, threonine and leucine, and so is not considered a complete protein on its own. Amaranth's protein is highly digestible, however, and the protein value increases when mixed with other cereal grain flours, making it a valuable non-animal source for vegetarians.

It is important to note that amaranth is considered a high glycemic food. This means it may cause blood sugar levels to spike. Avoiding the exclusive use of amaranth in dishes and instead using it in combinations of 25% or less will help lower any negative impact it may have on blood sugar and still enable you to benefit from its nutrition.

SERVINGS	COOKED AMOUNT (approx.)	AMOUNT OF AMARANTH AND WATER	
		Amaranth	Water
1	½ cup (125 mL)	¼ cup (60 mL)	¾ cup (175 mL)
2	1 cup (250 mL)	½ cup (125 mL)	1½ cups (375 mL)
3	1½ cups (375 mL)	¾ cup (175 mL)	2¼ cups (560 mL)
4	2 cups (500 mL)	1 cup (250 mL)	3 cups (750 mL)
5	2½ cups (625 mL)	1¼ cups (310 mL)	3¾ cups (925 mL)
6	3 cups (750 mL)	1½ cups (375 mL)	4½ cups (1 L + 125 mL)

Research has determined that eating amaranth can help lower blood pressure and cholesterol. Amaranth is a rich source of plant sterols, which reduce cholesterol levels by blocking its absorption in the intestine. Amaranth seeds contain a high amount of oil at 5% to 9%, which is thought to contribute to the cholesterol-lowering effect. These plant sterols may also help prevent cancer. Amaranth acts to inhibit inflammation and can also benefit those with a history of heart disease and stroke.

General Cooking Instructions

Amaranth Seeds

Bring the water and amaranth to a boil in an appropriate-sized saucepan. Reduce to a simmer, cover and cook for 15 minutes. Remove from the heat; drain or rinse in a fine-mesh strainer. Use as desired. This method provides the best flavor, nutrition retention, texture and flexibility for recipe use.

NOTE: You can leave the water in the saucepan after cooking and let it sit; it will become thick and slightly slimy but may still work for some of your recipes.

NUTRITIONAL PROFILE: Per Cooked Serving (½ cup/125 mL/123 g): Energy 125 calories; Protein 9 g; Carbohydrates 46 g; Dietary Fiber 5 g; Fat 4 g; Sugar 0 g; Cholesterol 0 mg; Sodium 15 mg (USDA National Nutrient Database for Standard Reference, 2012).

Popped Amaranth

Popped amaranth is a healthy and tasty snack, topping on salads or soups and in cereals and in snack bars. It even adds a unique crispness as a topping on sorbet or ice cream. See pages 70, 72, 73 and 164 for recipes that use popped amaranth.

1 Tbsp (15 mL) amaranth seeds =
¼ cup (60 mL) popped amaranth

Heat a dry 10- or 12-inch (25 or 30 cm) sauté pan with a lid over medium heat for at least 1½ minutes. The pan has reached the right temperature when you add seeds and they immediately start popping. Place 1 Tbsp (15 mL) amaranth in the pan and cover quickly. Move pan from side to side on the burner. The seeds should start popping. Remove pan from the heat when you can see that three-quarters of the amaranth has popped or when popping has slowed. Keep the lid on to pop any remaining seeds. Repeat with another tablespoon of amaranth if desired.

NOTE: Each stove heats differently and various pans conduct heat differently, so it may take slightly longer than 1½ minutes to reach optimum popping temperature. Also, it may take more than one attempt to perfect your timing and temperature to make puffs successfully.

Storage
Store uncooked seeds in a sealed container in a cool, dry, dark place, even in the refrigerator or freezer. Freezing in sealable freezer bags is recommended for storing unused flour, as amaranth is high in beneficial polyunsaturated fats that can become rancid, especially when seeds are ground. Cooked amaranth seeds will keep in a sealed container in the refrigerator for up to 3 days.

Buckwheat
FLAVOR: mild, nutty; *toasted or roasted*: earthy, rich, bold

TEXTURE: crunchy

FORMS: whole seeds or groats (hulled buckwheat), kasha (roasted groats), flour (light and dark), flakes, puffs

GLUTEN-FREE ✔

COMPLETE PROTEIN ✔

Cooking with Buckwheat
Buckwheat groats (the inner seeds of the kernel) can range from a light green to brown. Cooked, they can be used in salads, and they can be added to soups raw. Roasted groats, called kasha, can also be used the same way, but they have a different texture and richer, toasted flavor. Kasha does not cook the same way as buckwheat groats, so keep this in mind if using it in your recipes. Flakes and puffs can also be found in some markets and generally work well in most traditional recipes where flakes or puffs are used.

Other than pancakes, one of the foods we might most associate with buckwheat is Japanese soba noodles. Other common buckwheat uses include breakfast cereals, stir-fries, casseroles, crêpes, soups, salads, risotto, breads, tarts and muffins. As with other ancient grains, buckwheat does not always require cooking and groats can simply be soaked overnight, making them ideal for raw food diets.

Buckwheat flour can add nutrition and flavor to baking. Dark buckwheat flour contains unhulled buckwheat and therefore has a higher fiber content. Light buckwheat flour is made from groats, or hulled buckwheat, resulting in a lighter-colored flour and less fiber (without hulls). Using a combination of flours in baking, with no more than 50% buckwheat flour, can improve the texture of baked breads, making them softer and fluffier. In some locales, it can be more common to find buckwheat flour than other gluten-free flours.

You can toast buckwheat (groats) and buckwheat flour and flakes before cooking or baking (see toasting method on page 2). This releases and deepens the flavor, especially where you may want a toasted flavor, and adds a mild fragrance. Kasha is buckwheat groats that have already been roasted, so additional toasting is not necessary.

Nutrition
Buckwheat is rich in complex carbohydrates, fiber, magnesium and manganese. It is gluten-free and contains all the essential amino acids, making it a complete protein.

SERVINGS	COOKED AMOUNT (approx.)	AMOUNT OF BUCKWHEAT AND WATER	
		Buckwheat	Water
1	½ cup (125 mL)	¼ cup (60 mL)	½ cup (125 mL)
2	1 cup (250 mL)	½ cup (125 mL)	1 cup (250 mL)
4	2 cups (500 mL)	1 cup (250 mL)	2 cups (500 mL)
6	3 cups (750 mL)	1½ cups (375 mL)	3 cups (750 mL)

Eating buckwheat is thought to be a good preventive against cardiovascular disease and helps lower blood pressure and cholesterol. Magnesium helps to relax and open up blood vessels, improving circulation and blood flow. Buckwheat also contains flavonoids, considered anti-carcinogens. Simply put, they are phytonutrients, or beneficial plant chemicals, that act as antioxidants in the body, helping to clean and destroy cancer-causing toxins and free radicals. Buckwheat is also considered a low glycemic food, so it provides a handy alternative to traditional high glycemic foods such as rice and pasta. Its low impact on blood sugar makes it an ideal food for those with diabetes.

As with many whole grains and seeds high in complex carbohydrates and fiber, buckwheat is filling, suppresses appetite and digests more slowly, thus helping with weight loss. Buckwheat also contains prebiotic (insoluble) particles that stimulate probiotic (good) bacteria in the intestine.

General Cooking Instructions

Buckwheat (groats)

Bring the water and buckwheat to a boil in an appropriate-sized saucepan. Reduce to a simmer, cover and cook for 10 minutes (for salads) or 15 minutes (for fluffy grains). Remove from the heat and drain off any remaining liquid. Fluff with a fork. Use as desired. This method yields the best flavor, firm but tender texture (not mushy) and flexibility for recipe applications. If cooking toasted groats, or kasha, prepare by the same method but reduce the cooking time to 8 to 10 minutes.

NUTRITIONAL PROFILE: Per Cooked Serving (½ cup /125 mL/84 g): Energy 77 calories; Protein 3 g; Carbohydrates 17 g; Dietary Fiber 2 g; Fat 0.5 g; Sugar 1 g; Cholesterol 0 mg; Sodium 3 mg (USDA National Nutrient Database for Standard Reference, 2012).

Storage

Store buckwheat groats and kasha in a sealed container in a cool, dry cupboard. It is recommended that buckwheat flour be stored in the refrigerator for maximum freshness.

Chia

FLAVOR: mild, neutral, nutty
TEXTURE: seedy, gelatinous, tapioca-like
FORMS: whole seeds, ground; *colors:* black, brown, white
GLUTEN-FREE ✔
COMPLETE PROTEIN ✔

Cooking with Chia

No cooking required! Chia is a very low-maintenance superfood and can be eaten just the way you buy it. Ground or whole, black or white, chia seeds can be added to just about any recipe you choose. And a little chia goes a long way! Chia is a high-powered superfood and a single ounce (28 g) is considered a serving size, and even small amounts of chia can be used to enhance the nutrition of many different recipes.

Chia seeds can be prepared as a cereal or pudding or sprinkled in smaller portions into cereals, sauces, smoothies, salads, entrées or baking such as cookies and breads. Whole seeds can be added where they complement the texture of a recipe, such as rustic cookies or desserts, or they can be ground (using a coffee grinder) to create a finer texture that can be used when a smoother result is required, such as in sauces or puddings or as a soup or stew thickener.

Finely ground chia can serve multiple functions in recipes. Grinding 1 cup (250 mL) of whole chia seeds in a coffee grinder will produce 1¾ cups (425 mL) of finely ground chia. It can be used as part of a flour blend, as a butter or oil replacement or as a thickener. It can also serve as a binder in recipes, replacing eggs, xanthan gum or guar gum. Small but powerful, a single teaspoon (5 mL) can be all that's required, depending on the recipe. To replace 1 egg, mix ¼ cup water (60 mL) with 1 tsp (5 mL) ground chia or 1½ tsp (7 mL) whole chia seeds.

Chia acts like a sponge and holds moisture—approximately 10 times its weight! When soaked or mixed with liquids, often water, fruit juice or milk, it acquires a gel-like consistency. A thick gel made of chia mixed with water can work well as a substitute for a portion of the butter or oil in baking recipes, reducing saturated fat and adding beneficial essential fatty acids (fats that you have to consume because your body cannot make them on its own).

Nutrition

The benefits of eating chia can be had even by consuming small amounts. It is enzyme-rich and loaded with nutrition, including protein, fiber, calcium, magnesium, zinc, iron, phosphorus, potassium and antioxidants. It has the highest amount of omega-3 essential fatty acids of any plant-based food.

A tremendous source of energy, chia has had recent appeal among athletes, marathoners, bodybuilders and anyone with an active lifestyle. The essential fatty acids help boost metabolism, maintain and increase lean muscle, repair muscle tissue, support the heart and improve brain function. Chia also increases hydration and endurance and contains the trace mineral strontium, which aids in digestion and ensures efficient use of protein by the body. In addition, the omega-3 fatty acids help reduce inflammation and associated pain. Fiber-rich and easily digestible, chia helps you feel full, stabilizes blood sugar and is even thought to help with weight loss. The ease of digestion and chia's ability to absorb makes it useful for detoxification because, as it bulks up in the intestine, it whisks away toxins and cleanses the digestive system. Chia is also ideal for people with diabetes because, even with simple sugars, chia appears to block the quick breakdown of carbohydrates and slow the release of sugar in the blood. Chia supports good cardiovascular health, lowers cholesterol and blood pressure, and even improves immune function.

Chia Gel Yields

AMOUNT OF CHIA GEL (approx.)	AMOUNT OF CHIA AND WATER	
	Chia	Water
1½ Tbsp (22 mL)	1 tsp (5 mL)	1½ Tbsp (22 mL)
3 Tbsp (45 mL)	2 tsp (10 mL)	3 Tbsp (45 mL)
⅓ cup (80 mL)	4 tsp (20 mL)	6 Tbsp (90 mL)
½ cup (125 mL)	2 Tbsp (30 mL)	½ cup (125 mL)
¾ cup (175 mL)	8 tsp (40 mL)	¾ cup (175 mL)
1 cup (250 mL)	¼ cup (60 mL)	1 cup (250 mL)
2 cups (500 mL)	½ cup (125 mL)	2 cups (500 mL)

General Instructions

Chia Gel

Use as a butter or oil replacement for up to one-third of the butter or oil in your baking recipes.

MAKES 1 CUP (250 ML)

1 cup (250 mL) water
¼ cup (60 mL) ground chia seeds

Combine the water and ground chia in a small bowl. Gently stir with a fork to ensure seeds are evenly distributed. Cover and let sit in refrigerator for a minimum of 2 hours or overnight. Gel will be ready for use. Make as needed and store in a sealed container in the refrigerator for up to one week.

NUTRITIONAL PROFILE: Chia gel: Per Serving (2 Tbsp/ 30 mL): Energy 15 calories; Protein 1 g; Carbohydrates 2 g; Dietary Fiber 1 g; Fat 1 g; Sugar 0 g; Cholesterol 0 mg; Sodium 0 mg.

NUTRITIONAL PROFILE: Raw dry chia seeds: Per Serving (1 oz/28 g): Energy 140 calories; Protein 4 g; Carbohydrates 12 g; Dietary Fiber 11 g; Fat 9 g; Sugar 0 g; Cholesterol 0 mg; Sodium 5 mg (USDA National Nutrient Database for Standard Reference, 2012).

TIP: Need chia gel in a hurry? If you've ever been in the middle of a recipe, need chia gel and discover you don't have any, no problem! You don't have to wait for it to set. Just add ½ cup (125 mL) boiling water or liquid to 2 Tbsp (30 mL) ground chia and you will have ½ cup (125 mL) of chia gel instantly.

Toasting

Chia seeds, whole and ground, can be toasted before cooking or baking. This releases and deepens the flavor, especially where you may want a toasted flavor, and adds a very subtle, mildly fragrant aroma (see method on page 2).

Growing

Chia seeds can be grown as tiny living edible plants known as microgreens. These can be added to salads, sandwiches, smoothies—or just about anything you like. Find instructions for growing your own chia microgreens on page 8.

Storage

Chia's natural antioxidants help to promote longer shelf life of the stored seeds as well as anything you make with chia. Store unused seeds in a sealed container in a dry, cool location. Chia seeds kept this way should keep for a year or even longer.

Kañiwa

FLAVOR: slightly nutty, slightly sweet, milder than quinoa, earthy

TEXTURE: soft, crunchy, grainy

FORMS: whole seeds, flour

GLUTEN-FREE ✔

COMPLETE PROTEIN ✔

Cooking with Kañiwa

Kañiwa (pronounced kan-YEE-wa), also known as cañahua and cañawa, is often simply referred to as baby quinoa. This quinoa relation is even smaller than its relative, approximately one-third of the size of quinoa! It is red, gray, beige or light tan when uncooked but turns a brown-red color similar to red quinoa when cooked. It is known for its milder and sweeter taste compared to regular quinoa and has a soft and crunchy texture.

Unlike quinoa, kañiwa does not contain saponin, the substance that may sometimes cause a slightly bitter taste of quinoa. The good news is that if you're used to rinsing your quinoa, you don't need to rinse kañiwa. Just like quinoa, kañiwa has a little white endosperm that looks like a tiny sprout that pops out of the seed when it's cooked. Because it's so small, kañiwa is often mixed with quinoa or other ancient grains, sprouted, or added to salads, smoothies and sandwiches. It is also commonly made into porridge or breakfast cereal or added to vegetables in stir-fries or casseroles.

Kañiwa can also be used in the form of flour. It is used to fortify recipes and is often mixed with other gluten-free flour blends to enhance nutrition, flavor and texture. Up to 50% kañiwa flour can be used as part of a blend in many baking recipes, depending on the chemistry of other ingredients and the desired flavor and texture. Pastries, cakes and muffins, both sweet and savory, work well with kañiwa flour. Easily grind your own flour using a coffee grinder. Kañiwa seeds can also be popped like popcorn, producing a small, nutty, light brown puff that can be eaten alone, used as a topping or added to a snack mix.

Kañiwa seeds and flour can be toasted before cooking or baking. This releases and deepens the

Kañiwa seeds

SERVINGS	COOKED AMOUNT (approx.)	AMOUNT OF KAÑIWA AND WATER	
		Kañiwa	Water
1	½ cup (125 mL)	¼ cup (60 mL)	½ cup (125 mL)
2	1 cup (250 mL)	½ cup (125 mL)	1 cup (250 mL)
3	1½ cups (375 mL)	¾ cup (175 mL)	1½ cups (375 mL)
4	2 cups (500 mL)	1 cup (250 mL)	2 cups (500 mL)
5	2½ cups (625 mL)	1¼ cups (300 mL)	2½ cups (625 mL)
6	3 cups (750 mL)	1½ cups (375 mL)	3 cups (750 mL)

flavor, especially where you may want a toasted flavor, and adds a mildly fragrant aroma (see method on page 2).

Nutrition

Kañiwa is even higher in protein than quinoa and boasts a nutritional profile to impress any eater, whether interested in gluten-free, vegetarian, athletic performance or simply overall great health. Kañiwa's protein quality and ideal amino acid profile is comparable to quinoa's and similar to that of whole milk. Completely gluten-free, kañiwa is full of dietary fiber and naturally rich in calcium, zinc and iron. In addition, kañiwa contains unsaturated fatty acids that not only help increase the flexibility of cell membranes in the body but can help with a variety of health concerns, from diabetes to cancers. Kañiwa also has antioxidants that not only act as cancer-fighters but also help increase the products' shelf life. In addition to being a great everyday staple, the combination of high protein, fats and fiber make kañiwa valuable for losing weight, weaning babies, nourishing the elderly and improving digestion.

General Cooking Instructions

Bring the water and kañiwa to a boil in a medium saucepan. Reduce to a simmer, cover and cook for 10 minutes. Remove from the heat and drain any remaining water. The saucepan may remain on the stove, covered, to absorb additional water. Use as desired. This method provides the best flavor, texture and flexibility for recipe use.

Millet seeds

NUTRITIONAL PROFILE: Per Cooked Serving (½ cup/ 125 mL/67 g): Energy 265 calories; Protein 11g; Carbohydrates 44 g; Dietary Fiber 9 g; Fat 5 g; Sugar 0 g; Cholesterol 0 mg; Sodium 0 mg (Kañiwa Specifications Sheet, Specialty Commodities, Inc., Nov. 2011).

Buying and Storage

Kañiwa can be found in most of the same stores that sell quinoa or can easily be purchased online. It has a general shelf life of 2 years if kept in a cool, dry location in a tightly sealed container.

Millet

FLAVOR: mild, light, neutral

TEXTURE: fluffy, crunchy

FORMS: whole seeds, flour, puffs, flakes

GLUTEN-FREE ✔

COMPLETE PROTEIN ✗

Cooking with Millet

Often considered nothing more than bird seed, millet is now enjoying renewed popularity for its ancient grain status and gluten-free properties. It can be found in most of the same stores you can find other ancient grains and has likely been there all along. Different types of millet exist, but pearl millet is the most common in North America. The outer hull is removed for ease of eating and properly digesting the seeds.

Millet is a gluten-free alternative that can add variety in texture and taste. Prepared fluffy, sticky or creamy, millet seeds can be cooked longer with more water to achieve a fluffy result or cooked for a shorter time if you prefer crunchy. Ground before cooking, millet has an even creamier texture. Not just available as seeds, millet can also be found in flakes, flour and puff form.

For added texture and even quicker cooking, millet seeds can be presoaked overnight. Sprouted millet is also a favorite addition to salads, smoothies or sandwiches, providing added nutrition with living enzymes.

Millet seeds are delicious prepared as a breakfast cereal and can be cooked in combination with other grains or seeds. Millet's binding ability also makes it ideal for use in soups, stews and puddings, and its stickiness makes it perfect for patties or burgers. Millet flour is best used in combination with other flour blends in everything from biscuits and breads to cakes and cookies. You can also grind your own flour with a good blender or food processor. It is recommended that flour recipes use no more than one-third millet flour in a blend, but this can be increased, especially if you do not expect your recipe to rise much.

Millet seeds and flour can be toasted before cooking or baking. This releases and deepens the flavor, especially where you may want a toasted flavor, and adds a mildly fragrant aroma (see method on page 2).

Nutrition

A gluten-free energy source, millet also contains protein, but it is not a complete protein on its own and needs to be combined with beans or other foods to fill out the amino acid profile.

As with all ancient grains, millet is packed with fiber. In addition, millet offers B complex vitamins and is rich in minerals such as iron, magnesium, phosphorus, manganese, potassium, calcium, copper and zinc. Millet can help prevent heart disease, support blood vessels, reduce cholesterol and oxygenate the blood. Millet's low glycemic load makes it ideal for stabilizing blood sugar, thus

Millet Yields

SERVINGS	COOKED AMOUNT (approx.)	AMOUNT OF MILLET AND WATER	
		Millet	Water
1	½ cup (125 mL)	¼ cup (60 mL)	½ cup (125 mL)
2	1 cup (250 mL)	½ cup (125 mL)	1 cup (250 mL)
3	1½ cups (375 mL)	¾ cup (175 mL)	1½ cups (375 mL)
4	2 cups (500 mL)	1 cup (250 mL)	2 cups (500 mL)
5	2½ cups (625 mL)	¼ cup (300 mL)	2½ cups (625 mL)
6	3 cups (750 mL)	1½ cups (375 mL)	3 cups (750 mL)

helping to manage diabetes and reduce the onset of type 2 diabetes.

Millet has an alkaline effect in the body, digests easily and has good (prebiotic) bacteria to feed the probiotic bacteria in your intestine. The combination of millet's antioxidants (polyphenols) and overall nutrition can help prevent a range of diseases and illness.

Millet is rich in the amino acid tryptophan, which can increase serotonin levels, helping to calm your mood, reduce stress and improve sleep. It may also be beneficial for weight loss, as it is thought that tryptophan may also help reduce feelings of hunger and carbohydrate cravings.

General Cooking Instructions

Bring the water and millet to a boil in an appropriate-sized saucepan. Reduce to a simmer, cover and cook for 15 minutes. Remove from the heat and drain any remaining water. Fluff with a fork. Use as desired. This method provides the best flavor, texture (not mushy) and flexibility for recipe use.

NOTE: You can leave remaining water in the covered saucepan after cooking and let it sit. It will become mushy and overcooked but may be ideal for some of your recipes.

NUTRITIONAL PROFILE: Per Cooked Serving (½ cup/ 125 mL/87 g): Energy 105 calories; Protein 3 g; Carbohydrates 20 g; Dietary Fiber 1 g; Fat 1 g; Sugar 0 g; Cholesterol 0 mg; Sodium 0 mg (USDA National Nutrient Database for Standard Reference, 2012).

Oats

FLAVOR: light, mild, neutral, sweet
TEXTURE: *rolled oats*: soft, creamy, sticky, chewy; *steel-cut oats*: crunchy, chewy, coarse
FORMS: whole oat groats, rolled oats, steel-cut (Irish) oats, Scottish oats, oat bran
GLUTEN-FREE ✔
COMPLETE PROTEIN ✗

Cooking with Whole-Grain Oats

A traditional, satisfying comfort food for generations of children and adults, oats have a healthy history as breakfast porridge and baked in wholesome cookies. Oats are naturally gluten-free but may be contaminated if they are grown or processed in the same locations as gluten products.

Whole-grain oats can be bought in a wide variety of forms. Most commonly, regular (or old-fashioned) rolled oats are whole-grain oats that have been hulled (groats) and then steamed and rolled flat and sometimes lightly toasted. Quick-cooking or instant flakes have simply been rolled even thinner to produce a faster-cooking version. Scottish oats are groats that have been stone-ground, resulting in a variable texture ranging from chunks to powder and steel-cut oats are groats that have been sliced. Scottish and steel-cut versions provide various sizes of oat chunks that give us different texture options. A version of "quick" steel-cut oats is also available and is simply whole oats cut into flatter pieces to help reduce the cooking time. They are popular with those who want the same chunky oats but don't have time to cook traditional steel-cut oats. Oat bran is the outer layer of the whole grain oat. It is often eaten as a cereal on its own or simply added to baking or other dishes for its high content of soluble fiber.

Oat flour is a good alternative to regular flours or to combine with other flours in baking and can easily be ground at home using a blender. Grind whole-grain oats in a blender or food processor for 25 seconds or longer to get a powdery, soft oat flour. The finer the grind of oats, the better the binding ability. For most baking, up to 30% of the total flour can be oat flour. Flour can also be used in sauces or gravies and as a soup thickener.

Whole-grain oats have a delicately sweet flavor that is complementary to many other foods, making it a versatile ingredient to add to your ancient grain inventory. Sweet or savory, oats have a place beyond the obvious breakfasts, desserts and snacks, lunches and even dinners. Oats are used in cookies, bars, crackers, breads, cakes, muffins, breading for chicken or fish, sausage filler and as a binder in meatloaves, meatballs and beef or veggie burgers. Furthermore, rolled oats can even be eaten without being cooked at all, making great granola or cereal if time is a concern or if you're a raw food eater.

Nutrition

High in fiber, manganese, selenium, phosphorus, magnesium and zinc, oats have a long history of health benefits. Oats are known to improve digestion, reduce symptoms from coughs and colds, and enhance the skin when topically applied. Oats have also been found to reduce upper respiratory symptoms and the incidence of childhood asthma. A Finnish study showed that the earlier children were introduced to oats, the greater their chance of asthma was reduced. Beta glucans, or naturally occurring soluble sugars found in the cell walls of oats, have been found to have many health benefits. They help increase hormones that suppress appetite, increase immune function, prevent cancer, decrease tumors, reduce infection and speed healing, lower blood pressure and cholesterol, stabilize blood sugar and reduce the onset of type 2 diabetes.

Considered a lower glycemic food, soluble oat fiber reduces the speed of digestion, providing slow-release energy that can be used by the body instead of becoming quickly stored as body fat. The glycemic index of oats increases (and is thus more likely to cause spikes in blood sugar) as oats are processed further and soluble fiber is reduced.

Oat flakes

Rolled Oat Yields

SERVINGS	COOKED AMOUNT (approx.)	AMOUNT OF ROLLED OATS AND WATER	
		Rolled Oats	Water
1	½ cup (125 mL)	¼ cup (60 mL)	½ cup (125 mL)
2	1 cup (250 mL)	½ cup (125 mL)	1 cup (250 mL)
3	1½ cups (375 mL)	¾ cup (175 mL)	1½ cups (375 mL)

Steel-Cut Oat Yields

SERVINGS	COOKED AMOUNT (approx.)	AMOUNT OF STEEL-CUT OATS AND WATER	
		Steel-Cut Oats	Water
1	½ cup (125 mL)	3 Tbsp (45 mL)	½ cup (125 mL)
2	1 cup (250 mL)	⅓ cup (75 mL)	1 cup (250 mL)
3	1½ cups (375 mL)	½ cup (125 mL)	1½ cups (375 mL)

WHOLE OAT GROATS (UNROLLED) OR STEEL-CUT OATS

3-4 cups (750 mL–1 L) water (depending on desired creaminess)
1 cup (250 mL) steel-cut or whole oat groats

In a large saucepan, bring the water to a boil. Add the oats, stir and reduce to a simmer. Cover saucepan and cook until desired tenderness is reached—longer for softer oats and shorter for crunchier, stiffer oats. We recommend 20–30 minutes for steel-cut oats and 40–60 minutes for whole oat groats. (Drain off any remaining water in whole oats groats.)

OLD-FASHIONED (REGULAR OR LARGE-FLAKE) ROLLED OATS

Add 2 cups (500 mL) water to 1 cup (250 mL) rolled oats. Cooking time is 10 to 12 minutes, depending on desired tenderness. If you like extra-creamy cooked oats, add the oats to cold water, then bring to a boil.

General Cooking Instructions

As with most ancient grains and seeds, stovetop cooking works best.

Regardless of the type of oats you like best, if you want them fast and easy, oats can be prepared in advance and stored in the refrigerator for 3 to 4 days and eaten cold or quickly reheated for use.

Another easy way to prepare whole oat groats or steel-cut oats is to use a slow cooker.

NUTRITIONAL PROFILE: Per Cooked Serving (½ cup/ 125 mL/80 g): *Old-fashioned rolled oats:* Energy 160 calories; Protein 7 g; Carbohydrates 27 g; Dietary Fiber 4 g; Fat 2.5 g; Sugar 1 g; Cholesterol 0 mg; Sodium 0 mg.

NUTRITIONAL PROFILE: Per Cooked Serving (½ cup/ 125 mL/80 g): *Steel-cut oats:* Energy 280 calories; Protein 12 g; Carbohydrates 54 g; Dietary Fiber 8 g; Fat 5 g; Sugar 0 g; Cholesterol 0 mg; Sodium 0 mg (USDA National Nutrient Database for Standard Reference, 2012). Nutritional values are higher in steel-cut oats because they are larger chunks of the whole oat, but they are an even healthier option since they give your body the job of breaking them down.

Rolled oats, steel-cut oats and ground oats can be toasted before cooking or baking. This releases and deepens the flavor, especially where you may want a toasted flavor, and adds a mildly fragrant aroma (see method on page 2).

Quinoa

FLAVOR: nutty, neutral
TEXTURE: fluffy, crunchy, creamy
FORMS: whole seeds, flakes, flour, puffs; *colors:* red, black, white (golden)
GLUTEN-FREE ✔
COMPLETE PROTEIN ✔

Cooking with Quinoa

Quinoa has recently come into the superfood spotlight for its numerous health benefits and its versatility in cooking. A gluten-free, complete protein, quinoa seeds can be found in white, red and black and as flour, puffs and flakes. There are also more colors of quinoa currently being grown in South America that we will likely see in the world market in the near future.

Quinoa is often a replacement for rice and makes a great ingredient in soups, salads, casseroles, baked goods, desserts, breakfast cereals and baby foods. Quinoa more than triples in volume when cooked and has an adaptable flavor that lends to its versatility, complementing many flavors in many different cooking styles and recipe applications. Quinoa's texture can improve ordinary dishes and varies from al dente to fluffy, depending on the length of time it is cooked. It can be cooked in a variety of liquids, from water to soup stock and juices, and it can be cooked on the stovetop or in a slow cooker or rice steamer (rice cooker). It can be cooked in advance and stored in a sealed container in the refrigerator for up to 5 days and added to a variety of meal preparations.

Both quinoa seeds and flour can be used as a thickener in soups and sauces. For example, whole seeds can simply be added to soups or cooked and puréed to create a thicker soup without the addition of heavy cream. Quinoa seeds can also be used raw, ground or sprouted, in salads, sandwiches or breakfast smoothies, which makes it especially popular for raw food eaters. Quinoa flour can be used in baking and is useful in flour blends, where it can help absorb and hold liquid, improving moistness and providing a fluffy, soft texture. Combining quinoa flour with other flours—such as amaranth, buckwheat, kañiwa, millet, oat, sorghum, teff, tapioca, almond, coconut and rice flours— makes for a wide range of options that allow you to create impressive dishes that meet different nutritional requirements and have wonderfully complex

SERVINGS	COOKED AMOUNT (approx.)	AMOUNT OF QUINOA AND WATER	
		Quinoa	Water
1	1 cup (250 mL)	⅓ cup (75 mL)	⅔ cup (150 mL)
2	2 cups (500 mL)	⅔ cup (150 mL)	1⅓ cups (325 mL)
3	3 cups (750 mL)	1 cup (250 mL)	2 cups (500 mL)

flavors. Quinoa flakes can also be widely found and make a delicious breakfast cereal or a coating for meats and vegetables and can also be used in baking or as a dessert ingredient. Quinoa seeds, flour and flakes can all be toasted before cooking or baking. This releases and deepens the flavor, especially where you may want a toasted flavor, and adds a mildly fragrant aroma (see method on page 2).

Some people prefer to rinse quinoa seeds before cooking. This helps eliminate any remaining bitter flavor on the seeds caused by saponins, the plant's naturally occurring pesticide and insecticide, but most packaged quinoa has already been washed repeatedly and does not require additional washing. If you purchase your quinoa in bulk or direct from growers, however, you may find that washing is required.

To rinse, simply hold for a few minutes under running water in a strainer or in a piece of pantyhose or nylon stocking. To rinse it even more thoroughly, it can be soaked and then rinsed. For a comprehensive guide to quinoa with more specific instructions and troubleshooting tips on rinsing, sprouting and overall cooking of quinoa, we recommend our bestselling book, *Quinoa Revolution: Over 150 Healthy, Great-Tasting Recipes Under 500 Calories.*

Nutrition

Quinoa has been identified as one of the world's healthiest foods. A favorite of vegetarians, quinoa is a non-animal protein source that contains all nine essential amino acids, making it a complete protein. Quinoa is also rich in minerals such as iron, phosphorus, magnesium, calcium and potassium, and vitamins such as vitamin E, riboflavin and folate.

Since it is not at all related to wheat, quinoa is a valuable gluten-free food that is a favorite of people with food allergies and digestive intolerances, especially those affected by celiac disease, Crohn's disease or colitis. It is also recommended in the gluten-free diets for autistic children or those with attention deficit hyperactivity disorder (ADHD).

Often used in weight loss diets, quinoa has a low glycemic index and is high in complex carbohydrates, which means that sugars are not quickly converted to fats but instead used by the body as slow-releasing energy. In fact, quinoa has a wide range of health benefits, including building and repairing muscle and preventing bone loss. Easily digestible, quinoa's nutrients are readily absorbed by the body, making it an ideal food for athletes and overall health and fitness. In addition, quinoa is rich in histadine, an essential amino acid known to support human growth and development. The complete amino acid profile of quinoa, including histidine, makes it naturally superior for nourishing children, and especially weaning babies. Quinoa is also high in linolenic acid, an essential fatty acid proven to optimize immune function, and is high in manganese and copper, which makes it rich in antioxidants that help eliminate toxins and free radicals that may ultimately lead to disease and even increase the shelf life of the product. Quinoa has been demonstrated to help reduce high blood pressure and improve cardiovascular functioning and, because it is full of powerful phytonutrients, is thought to help prevent a variety of illnesses, including everything from cancers to gallstones and diabetes.

General Cooking Instructions

2 cups (250 mL) water
1 cup (250 mL) quinoa seeds

Combine the water and quinoa in a medium saucepan and bring to a boil. Reduce to a simmer, cover and cook for 15 minutes. Cooked quinoa is translucent and a tiny white tail-like sprout uncurls from the outside of the seed.

NOTE: Depending on desired tenderness, you may wish to cook quinoa with only 1½ cups (375 mL) water for every 1 cup (250 mL) of seeds. With less water, the result will be slightly chewier, but this can be a good option, especially for salads. The method is the same. Bring the water and quinoa to a boil in a medium saucepan, then cover and reduce to a simmer for 10 minutes. Turn the heat off and let sit, covered, for an additional 3 to 4 minutes or until preferred doneness is reached.

NUTRITIONAL PROFILE: Per Cooked Serving (1 cup/ 250 mL/185 g): Energy 222 calories; Protein 8.1 g; Carbohydrates 39 g; Dietary Fiber 5.2 g; Fat 3.6 g; Sugar 0 g; Cholesterol 0 mg; Sodium 13 mg (USDA National Nutrient Database for Standard Reference, 2012).

Sprouting Quinoa

Of all the ancient grains, quinoa seeds make some of the best sprouts. They germinate quickly, in 2 to 4 hours, and are a great way to eat living enzymes you can grow all on your own—year-round. For sprouting instructions, see page 5.

Sorghum

FLAVOR: neutral, wheat-like, nutty, sweet
TEXTURE: crunchy, fluffy
FORMS: whole grains, flour
GLUTEN-FREE ✔
COMPLETE PROTEIN ✗

Cooking with Sorghum

Sorghum is a grain mainly grown for its edible seeds, though some varieties are grown for the stalks, which are used to make molasses, sugar and syrup. Sorghum grains can be white or red and are similar in size and shape to millet. Although sorghum does not have as much protein quality as some of the other ancient grains, it still contains protein and makes a nutritious, unique addition to gluten-free whole-grain recipes. It is also not a complete protein, but adding foods that are rich in sorghum's only limited amino acid, lysine, will make it one. Foods rich in lysine include amaranth, mushrooms, corn, cheese, eggs, nuts and legumes such as beans, peas and lentils. Sorghum grains have edible

SERVINGS	COOKED AMOUNT (approx.)	AMOUNT OF SORGHUM AND WATER	
		Sorghum	Water
1	½ cup (125 mL)	3 Tbsp (45 mL)	⅔ cup (150 mL)
2	1 cup (250 mL)	⅓ cup + 1 Tbsp (90 mL)	1⅓ cups (300 mL)
3	1½ cups (375 mL)	½ cup + 2 tsp (135 mL)	2 cups (500 mL)
4	2 cups (500 mL)	¾ cup + 1 tsp (180 mL)	2⅔ cups (650 mL)
5	2½ cups (625 mL)	¾ cup + 3 Tbsp (225 mL)	3⅓ cups (825 mL)

hulls, so the hulls are often left intact, retaining nutrients and fiber. Cooked sorghum grains can be prepared as a breakfast porridge, used as a replacement for rice in side dishes, soups, and stir-fries or popped much like popped corn. Sorghum flour can enhance the texture of baked goods and add variety to any of the other gluten-free flours you use. We recommend using no more than one-third as part of a flour blend, as it can result in dry baked goods. Greater amounts of sorghum flour require more eggs, oil or moisture. Ascorbic acid or apple cider vinegar may also improve the volume of dough made with sorghum flour. Sorghum flour is frequently used in recipes such as pancakes, bread doughs, waffles, muffins, cookies and pasta. It is a great option for thickening liquids to make sauces, soups, stews and gravies. It is also ideal for puddings because it continues to thicken as it cools and adds a touch of sweet flavor.

Of all the gluten-free ancient grains used in this book, sorghum takes the longest to cook. If you find that you like adding sorghum to recipes, it is wise to cook a batch in advance to be used throughout your week.

Sorghum grains and flour can be toasted before cooking or baking. This releases and deepens the flavor, especially where you may want a toasted flavor, and adds a mildly fragrant aroma (see method on page 2). Be watchful, as sorghum can burn quickly.

Nutrition

Sorghum is high in fiber and protein and contains omega-3 and omega-6 fatty acids, B complex vitamins and minerals such as phosphorus, calcium and potassium. In many countries, sorghum is used for a wide range of medicinal benefits, including aiding digestion, soothing skin conditions and acting as a diuretic. It has high antioxidant properties, helping to defend the body against free radicals and toxins that may cause illness or disease. Policosanols, an extract of the plant wax from sorghum, have been found to benefit cardiovascular health and lower cholesterol. Research has also shown sorghum to prevent diabetes and ward off resistance to insulin. Recent studies on sorghum also indicate that it can prevent the growth of cancerous tumors, especially those related to skin cancer.

General Cooking Instructions

3 cups (750 mL) water
1 cup (250 mL) sorghum grains

Combine the water and sorghum in a medium saucepan and bring to a boil. Reduce to a simmer, cover and cook for 25 to 30 minutes, then let sit, covered, for an additional 15 minutes. Any remaining water can be drained off. Cooked sorghum will be soft and slightly chewy. Cooking times can be adjusted according to cooked texture preference.

NUTRITIONAL PROFILE: Per Cooked Serving (½ cup/ 125 mL/96 g): Energy 330 calories; Protein 11 g; Carbohydrates 72 g; Dietary Fiber 6 g; Fat 3 g; Sugar 0 g; Cholesterol 0 mg; Sodium 5 mg (USDA National Nutrient Database for Standard Reference, 2012).

Popped Sorghum

Popped sorghum is useful as a topping on salads or soups, in cereals and in snack bars. They even add a unique crispness as a topping on sorbet or ice cream. See pages 70, 72, 73 and 164 for recipes that use popped sorghum.

> 1 Tbsp (15 mL) sorghum grains =
> ¼ cup (60 mL) popped sorghum

Heat a dry 10- or 12-inch (25 or 30 cm) sauté pan with lid over medium heat for at least 1½ minutes. The pan has reached the right temperature when you add grains and they immediately start popping. Place 1 Tbsp (15 mL) sorghum grains in the pan and cover quickly. Move pan from side to side on the burner. The grains should start popping. Remove pan from the heat when you can see that three-quarters of the sorghum has popped or when popping has slowed. Keep the lid on to pop any remaining grains. Repeat with another tablespoon of sorghum if desired.

NOTE: Each type of stove heats differently and various pans conduct heat differently, so it may take slightly longer than 1½ minutes to reach optimum popping temperature. Also, it may take more than one attempt to perfect your timing and temperature to successfully pop sorghum.

Sprouting and Soaking Sorghum

Sorghum grains are not recommended for sprouting or soaking, as they have been known to generate high levels of cyanide during these processes.

Buying and Storage

Whole sorghum can be found in specialty stores, health food stores, some grocery stores and online. Terrific for its nutrition and applications in today's high demand for gluten-free baking, sorghum flour can also be found in grocery stores, health food stores and bulk food stores. Often called sweet sorghum flour, it is a pale cream color and has a taste similar to wheat flour but with a subtle nutty flavor and a hint of sweetness.

Store unused sorghum grains in a sealed container in a dark, dry cupboard. Store flour in a sealed container in the refrigerator or freezer to ensure maximum freshness.

Teff

FLAVOR: *lighter teff*: nutty, sweet, light; *darker teff*: sweet, earthy, nutty, molasses-like
TEXTURE: gelatinous, crunchy
FORMS: whole seeds, flour
GLUTEN-FREE ✔
COMPLETE PROTEIN ✔

SERVINGS	COOKED AMOUNT (approx.)	AMOUNT OF TEFF AND WATER	
		Teff	Water
1	½ cup (125 mL)	¼ cup (60 mL)	¾ cup (175 mL)
2	1 cup (250 mL)	½ cup (125 mL)	1½ cups (375 mL)
3	1½ cups (375 mL)	¾ cup (175 mL)	2¼ cups (550 mL)
4	2 cups (500 mL)	1 cup (250 mL)	3 cups (750 mL)
5	2½ cups (625 mL)	1¼ cups (300 mL)	3¾ cups (925 mL)
6	3 cups (750 mL)	1½ cups (375 mL)	4½ cups (1.125 L)

Cooking with Teff

Despite teff's tiny size, it is actually not a seed but a grain. Too small to be hulled, it is eaten with the outermost, digestible layer completely intact. Convenient and easy, its tiny size means it cooks quickly. It is gluten-free, a complete protein, and grains can range in color from white to a dark reddish brown. The flavor of light-colored teff has been compared to hazelnuts and the taste of the darker version of teff is often compared to that of molasses. In some cases, teff's flavor can overpower, so using it in appropriate recipes, combinations and proportions is important.

When combined with liquid, teff has gel-like properties that make it useful as a replacement for butter or oil in some recipes or as a thickener in soups and sauces. Teff can be found in its grain form and in flour form. In Ethiopia, teff is used in a traditional fermented flatbread called *injera*. In North America, teff grains are most often prepared as a breakfast cereal, and the flour is used in pancakes, soups, breads and flatbreads, cakes and pastries, especially as part of mixed flour blends. The recommended amount of teff in a flour blend is approximately 25%, with potato starch or xanthan gum added where additional binding properties are required.

Teff seeds and flour can be toasted before cooking or baking. This releases and deepens the flavor, especially where you may want a toasted flavor, and adds a mildly fragrant aroma (see method on page 2).

Nutrition

Teff is another gluten-free, complete-protein superfood. It is rich in calcium, phosphorus, copper and potassium and also contains vitamin C, which is fairly unique among grains. It contains energy-rich complex carbohydrates and has a low glycemic index. Distance runners from African countries have claimed that eating teff provides them with the energy and stamina to run long distances.

Teff is naturally rich in resistant starch. A type of dietary fiber, resistant starch has the benefits of both insoluble and soluble fiber. Thought to make foods lower-calorie, resistant starch is thought to *resist* being absorbed into the body as sugar and instead behaves like dietary fiber, or roughage.

Resistant starch benefits digestion, stabilizes blood sugar and helps to burn body fat by increasing the efficiency of body metabolism. For these reasons, teff may help with weight loss, as resistant starch also helps to curb appetite.

One of the most significant benefits of teff may be the naturally occurring high concentrations of resistant starches that act as anti-carcinogens. Especially beneficial for colorectal cancer, resistant starches produce a fatty acid called butyrate that keeps colon cells healthy by preventing tumor growth, and it has been found that they even actively terminate cancer cells in the colon. Beneficial for eye health, teff may also prevent macular degeneration in aging adults.

General Cooking Instructions

Methods for cooking teff can vary depending on how you prefer to eat it. More liquid is added for a creamier texture and less liquid for a crunchier, seedier texture.

Bring the water and teff to a boil in an appropriate-sized saucepan. Reduce to a simmer, cover and cook for 15 minutes. Remove from the heat and drain or rinse in a fine-mesh strainer. Use as desired. This method will provide the best flavor, texture and flexibility for recipe use.

NOTE: You can leave remaining water in the saucepan after cooking and let it sit. It will be thick and slightly slimy, but this may work for some of your recipes.

NUTRITIONAL PROFILE: Per Cooked Serving (½ cup/ 125 mL/126 g): Energy 130 calories; Protein 5 g; Carbohydrates 25 g; Dietary Fiber 4 g; Fat 1 g; Sugar 0 g; Cholesterol 0 mg; Sodium 10 mg (USDA National Nutrient Database for Standard Reference, 2012).

Sprouting Teff

Teff can also be sprouted. For instructions on how to do this yourself, see page 5.

Storage

Uncooked teff seeds and flour should be stored in a cool, dry, dark location in a sealed container such as glass. Ground flour can be kept in the cupboard but has a much longer shelf life if stored in the refrigerator or freezer. Store cooked teff in a sealed container in the refrigerator for 2 to 3 days.

Teff grains

NUTRITIONAL VALUES OF GLUTEN-FREE ANCIENT GRAINS

PER ½-CUP (125 ML) SERVING, COOKED GRAINS OR SEEDS	CALORIES	PROTEIN (G)	CARBS (G)	FIBER (G)	FAT (G)	SUGAR (G)	CHOLESTEROL (MG)	SODIUM (MG)
Amaranth	125	4.7	23	2.6	1.9	0	0	7
Buckwheat	77	2.8	17	2.3	0.5	1	0	0
Chia (uncooked)	450	15	39	32	28	0	0	15
Kañiwa	133	5	33	4	3	0	0	0
Millet	105	3	21	1	0	0	0	0
Oats – regular (old-fashioned rolled)	83	3	14	2	1.8	0.3	0	5
Oats – steel-cut	280	10	54	8	4	0	0	0
Quinoa	111	4	19	2.6	1.8	0	0	6
Sorghum	325	11	72	6	3	0	0	6
Teff	127	5	25	3.4	1	0	0	10

SOURCES: *USDA National Nutrient Database for Standard Reference, 2012; Kañiwa Specifications Sheet, Specialty Commodities, Inc., 2011.*

GLUTEN AND PROTEIN QUALITY IN ANCIENT GRAINS AND SEEDS

	TYPE	GLUTEN	PROTEIN
Amaranth	Seed	Gluten-Free	Incomplete
Buckwheat	Seed	Gluten-Free	Complete
Chia	Seed	Gluten-Free	Complete
Kañiwa	Seed	Gluten-Free	Complete
Millet	Seed	Gluten-Free	Incomplete
Oats	Grain	Gluten-Free	Incomplete
Quinoa	Seed	Gluten-Free	Complete
Sorghum	Grain	Gluten-Free	Incomplete
Teff	Grain	Gluten-Free	Complete

BREAKFAST

No routine here! Breakfast is never boring with ancient grains. This chapter will provide you with tasty alternatives to invigorate your regular breakfast routine. These uncomplicated recipes are delicious enough to ensure they find space in your busy day and will energize you enough to keep you coming back for more. Lemon Cashew Ginger Ancient Grain Granola (page 50) and Pumpkin Spice Steel-Cut Oats (page 48) will give you a healthy start on daily nutrients, and Toasted Coconut Fruit Salad with Quinoa & Pineapple Lime Dressing (page 62) tastes good enough to sneak its way into your lunch and dinner too. Just need a small dose? A dollop of Raspberry Chia Jam (page 35) can make the perfect surprise on top of plain yogurt, hot cereal, crêpes, waffles or a short stack of pancakes. Entertaining or preparing a brunch? Try Prosciutto & Kale Kañiwa Frittata with Romano Cheese (page 65) and White Chocolate Raspberry Sorghum & Oat Scones (page 61). Whether you need to prepare in advance or are inspired when you roll out of bed, these recipes are sure to get you in the mood for breakfast!

STRAWBERRY & MANGO QUINOA SPROUT SMOOTHIE

SERVES 2

The delicious blend of frozen strawberries and mangos adds a refreshing tropical flavor to breakfast. We recommend substituting raspberries for the strawberries for another great-tasting option.

2/3 cup (150 mL) frozen or fresh strawberries

2/3 cup (150 mL) frozen or fresh mango

1/2 cup (125 mL) unsweetened (or sweetened) cranberry juice

1/2 cup (125 mL) water

1/2 cup (125 mL) quinoa sprouts

1/3 cup (75 mL) vanilla yogurt (optional)

1 tsp (5 mL) chia seeds (optional)

Place the strawberries, mango, cranberry juice, water, sprouts, yogurt and chia seeds in a blender. Purée until smooth. Serve.

PER SERVING: Energy 100 calories; Protein 2 g; Carbohydrates 25 g; Dietary Fiber 3 g; Fat 0 g; Sugar 17 g; Cholesterol 0 mg; Sodium 0 mg.

> Any type of sprout would be an option in this smoothie.

CHOCOLATE BANANA & PEANUT BUTTER AMARANTH SMOOTHIE

SERVES 2

Chocolate, bananas and peanut butter mingle with your favorite ancient grain (or whatever happens to be left over in the refrigerator) for a satisfying breakfast shake that is good for your waistline.

2/3 cup (150 mL) vanilla yogurt

1/2 medium banana (1/4 to 1/3 cup/60 to 75 mL)

1/2 cup (125 mL) 1% milk

1/4 cup (60 mL) cooked amaranth seeds

1 tsp (5 mL) unsweetened cocoa powder

2 Tbsp (30 mL) natural peanut butter

Combine the yogurt, banana, milk, amaranth, cocoa and peanut butter in a blender and purée until smooth. Serve.

PER SERVING: Energy 230 calories; Protein 11 g; Carbohydrates 25 g; Dietary Fiber 3 g; Fat 10 g; Sugar 13 g; Cholesterol 10 mg; Sodium 140 mg.

> For variation, substitute quinoa, buckwheat, teff, steel-cut oats or kañiwa for the amaranth.

RASPBERRY CHIA JAM

MAKES 1¹/₂ CUPS (375 ML), 12 SERVINGS (2 TBSP/30 ML EACH)

A tasty and sweet raspberry jam that is chock-full of super chia nutrition and a great addition on top of breakfast cereals, yogurt, pancakes, waffles, crêpes and even dessert cakes, ice cream and puddings. It's an easy way to inject a dose of beneficial omega-3s and overall superior nourishment (and an aid to digestion) into your day—but even your kids won't recognize this as anything but yummy! Jam will keep for up to 7 days in a sealed container in the refrigerator.

Combine the water and sugar in a medium bowl and stir to begin to dissolve sugar. Add ground chia and gently stir with a fork to ensure it is evenly distributed. Combine with raspberries and purée mixture with a hand blender or in a food processor until well combined. (A potato masher and a bit of muscle works too.)

Cover and let sit in refrigerator for a minimum of 2 hours or overnight. Topping will be ready for use. Serve cold.

¼ cup (60 mL) water
¼ cup (60 mL) white or organic cane sugar
¼ cup (60 mL) ground white chia seeds
1 cup (250 ml) frozen or fresh raspberries

PER SERVING: Energy 40 calories; Protein 1 g; Carbohydrates 7 g; Dietary Fiber 2 g; Fat 1 g; Sugar 4 g; Cholesterol 0 mg; Sodium 0 mg.

Heat it up! This sauce can be gently warmed over low heat if you prefer a warm topping.

Chocolate Banana & Peanut
Butter Amaranth Smoothie

Strawberry & Mango
Quinoa Sprout Smoothie

CHIA CHAI SORGHUM CEREAL

SERVES 2

Enjoy the warm, peppery, sweet cinnamon flavor of chai in this creamy hot cereal enriched with chia.

1½ cups (375 mL) water
½ cup (125 mL) sorghum grains
1 cup (250 mL) 1% milk (or light coconut, almond or rice milk)
1 chai tea bag
1 large egg white
1 to 2 Tbsp (15 to 30 mL) honey or pure maple syrup
½ tsp (2 mL) pure vanilla extract
1 Tbsp (15 mL) chia seeds

Combine the water and sorghum in a medium saucepan. Bring to a simmer, covered, on medium-low heat for 50 minutes or until the sorghum is tender. Drain any remaining water. Add the milk and the tea bag; simmer, uncovered, for 5 minutes.

Whisk the egg white in a small bowl with 1 Tbsp (15 mL) hot cereal to temper the egg. Repeat with an additional 5 Tbsp (75 mL) cereal until the egg white is no longer noticeable and fully incorporated. Stir egg mixture into the saucepan and cook for 1 minute, until the cereal has thickened slightly. Remove the tea bag. Stir in the honey, vanilla and chia. Serve with your choice of sweetener or with milk if desired.

PER SERVING: Energy 310 calories; Protein 14 g; Carbohydrates 54 g; Dietary Fiber 5 g; Fat 7 g; Sugar 14 g; Cholesterol 100 mg; Sodium 100 mg.

- 1½ cups (375 mL) cooked quinoa, kañiwa, millet, amaranth or teff can easily be substituted for sorghum.
- Switch it up by using a chocolate chai tea bag. Serve with a small amount of dark chocolate grated on top instead of adding a sweetener.
- Replace ¼ cup (60 mL) of sorghum with ¼ cup (60 mL) amaranth to make it a complete protein.

WARM GINGERBREAD TEFF CEREAL

SERVES 2

Looking for something a little different for breakfast? The combination of ginger, cinnamon, molasses and brown sugar makes a yummy, sweet and healthy gingerbread-inspired cereal!

Combine the water and teff in a medium saucepan and stir in the molasses, cinnamon and ginger. Bring to a boil, then reduce to a simmer and cover. Cook for 20 minutes, stirring occasionally. Remove from the heat. Stir in the brown sugar and milk. Serve.

PER SERVING: Energy 240 calories; Protein 7 g; Carbohydrates 51 g; Dietary Fiber 4 g; Fat 1 g; Sugar 14 g; Cholesterol 0 mg; Sodium 25 mg.

1½ cups (375 mL) water
½ cup (125 mL) teff grains
2 tsp (10 mL) fancy molasses
¾ tsp (3 mL) cinnamon
Pinch of ground ginger
2 Tbsp (30 mL) brown sugar
2 Tbsp (30 mL) 1% milk

Teff grains

CREAMY VANILLA FIG MILLET CEREAL

SERVES 2

Having a healthy breakfast doesn't have to mean eating the same breakfast every day. After you try this one, we're sure you'll find a way to work it into your schedule. Creamy millet, coconut milk and sweet figs with a touch of vanilla are sure to make you completely forget about all the nutrition you're getting.

1½ cups (375 mL) water

⅔ cup (150 mL) millet seeds

½ cup (125 mL) light coconut milk

5 dried figs (any type), chopped

1½ tsp (7 mL) pure vanilla extract

1 tsp (5 mL) honey or pure
    maple syrup

Bring the water and millet to a boil in a medium saucepan. Cover, reduce to a simmer and cook for 15 minutes. Remove the lid; stir in the milk and figs. Simmer, uncovered, until the milk has reduced and cereal is creamy. Stir in the vanilla and honey. Divide between two bowls and serve.

PER SERVING: Energy 350 calories; Protein 9 g; Carbohydrates 65 g; Dietary Fiber 13 g; Fat 7 g; Sugar 12 g; Cholesterol 0 mg; Sodium 20 mg.

Instead of light coconut milk, you could also use almond, soy or rice milk.

SPICED APPLE CRANBERRY BUCKWHEAT CEREAL

SERVES 2

Knock out the same old breakfast routine with yummy cereal full of warm spices and fruit—indulge in the fabulous flavors of grains mixed with apples, cranberries, cinnamon, nutmeg and cloves in this quick and easy breakfast.

1 cup (250 mL) water
½ cup (125 mL) unsweetened apple juice
¼ cup (60 mL) quinoa seeds
¼ cup (60 mL) buckwheat groats
3 Tbsp (45 mL) chopped dried apple
1 Tbsp (15 mL) dried sweetened cranberries or raisins
½ tsp (2 mL) cinnamon
Pinch of nutmeg
Pinch of ground cloves
2 tsp (10 mL) honey or pure maple syrup (optional)
½ cup (125 mL) milk (optional)

Combine the water, juice, quinoa, buckwheat, apple, cranberries, cinnamon, nutmeg, and cloves in a medium saucepan and bring to a boil. Reduce to a simmer, cover and cook for 15 minutes. Remove from the heat, stir and serve with honey and milk if desired.

PER SERVING: Energy 220 calories; Protein 6 g; Carbohydrates 45 g; Dietary Fiber 4 g; Fat 2 g; Sugar 14 g; Cholesterol 0 mg; Sodium 35 mg.

> This cereal can also be made with ¼ cup (60 mL) millet, amaranth or teff in place of buckwheat.

RAISIN OATMEAL COOKIE CEREAL

SERVES 2

Here is a breakfast cereal based on a traditional cookie favorite. Steel-cut oats are toasted and cooked with warm cinnamon, plump raisins and a hint of vanilla.

⅔ cup (150 mL) steel-cut oats
2 cups (500 mL) water
3 Tbsp (45 mL) raisins
½ tsp (2 mL) cinnamon
1 tsp (5 mL) butter (optional)
2 tsp (10 mL) pure vanilla extract
1 Tbsp (15 mL) brown sugar, honey or pure maple syrup

Preheat a sauté pan or saucepan with a lid on medium-low heat. Place the steel-cut oats in the pan and toast, stirring frequently, for about 4 minutes, until fragrant and toasted. Pour in the water, raisins and cinnamon and bring to a boil. Reduce to a simmer, cover and cook for 20 minutes or until the oats are tender. Remove the lid and cook for another 2 to 5 minutes until the water has reduced. Stir in the butter (if using), vanilla and brown sugar. Serve.

PER SERVING: Energy 260 calories; Protein 8 g; Carbohydrates 52 g; Dietary Fiber 6 g; Fat 3.5 g; Sugar 13 g; Cholesterol 0 mg; Sodium 10 mg.

FIVE-MINUTE SUPERCEREAL

SERVES 2

Need something fast and simple for breakfast? Try our five-minute supercereal with the basic flavors of cinnamon and vanilla to get you started. Customize it by adding your choice of fruit and nuts. Don't skip breakfast! If you're in a rush, take it to work. Simply add boiling water to the cereal and let sit, covered, for 5 to 10 minutes until tender.

Combine the four ancient grains in a designated coffee grinder or blender and pulse until grains are in small meal-sized pieces. Remove ½ cup (125 mL) ground grains and store the remainder for future breakfasts.

Place the measured grains in a medium saucepan. Stir in water, milk, cinnamon and any fruit or nuts you desire. Bring to a boil and stir. Reduce to a simmer. Do not cover; stir again at 2½ minutes. At 5 minutes, remove from the heat, stir in vanilla and replace lid until ready to serve. Serve with your choice of sweetener and additional milk if desired.

PER SERVING: Energy 200 calories; Protein 8 g; Carbohydrates 36 g; Dietary Fiber 5 g; Fat 3 g; Sugar 3 g; Cholesterol 5 mg; Sodium 35 mg.

¼ cup (60 mL) quinoa seeds

2 Tbsp (30 mL) millet seeds

2 Tbsp (30 mL) buckwheat groats

1½ tsp (7 mL) amaranth seeds

1 cup (250 mL) water

½ cup (250 mL) 1% milk, milk substitute or light coconut milk

½ tsp (2 mL) cinnamon

½ tsp (2 mL) pure vanilla extract

Any combination of sweeteners (brown sugar, pure maple syrup, honey) and dried fruit (raisins, currants, cranberries) or nuts (almonds, walnuts, peanuts) that you prefer

MASON JAR ANCIENT GRAIN BREAKFAST

SERVES 1

Delicious and convenient! Fill a mason jar with a few simple ingredients and your breakfast will be waiting and ready to eat when you wake up in the morning. Choose your favorite ancient grains, fruits and spices. Customize this breakfast to your tastes, nutritional requirements and the grains you have on hand. Simply satisfying!

Measure oats, amaranth, buckwheat and teff into the appropriate-sized mason jar. Add raisins, chia and cinnamon. Pour boiling water into the jar. Screw on the lid tightly and shake. If time permits, set jar on the counter for 15 to 20 minutes. Shake again and place in the refrigerator for 7 hours or more.

Remove from the refrigerator and reheat in a saucepan or microwave until desired temperature is reached. Stir in the milk and sprinkle with nuts and sweetener if desired. Serve.

PER SERVING (*SMALL*): Energy 210 calories; Protein 7 g; Carbohydrates 42 g; Dietary Fiber 6 g; Fat 3.5 g; Sugar 9 g; Cholesterol 0 mg; Sodium 10 mg.

PER SERVING (*BIG*): Energy 270 calories; Protein 9 g; Carbohydrates 53 g; Dietary Fiber 7 g; Fat 4.5 g; Sugar 11 g; Cholesterol 0 mg; Sodium 10 mg.

> For an alternative, top with fresh fruit such as raspberries, blueberries or even peaches instead of using dried fruit.

SMALL BREAKFAST

½-pint (1 cup/250 mL) mason jar with lid

2 Tbsp (30 mL) steel-cut oats

1 Tbsp (15 ml) amaranth seeds

1 Tbsp (15 mL) buckwheat groats

1½ Tbsp (22 mL) raisins

1 tsp (5 mL) chia seeds

Pinch of cinnamon

¾ cup (175 mL) boiling water

2 Tbsp (30 mL) milk (optional)

1 Tbsp (15 mL) nuts, your choice (optional)

BIG BREAKFAST

1-pint (2 cups/500 mL) mason jar with lid

2 Tbsp (30 mL) steel-cut oats

2 Tbsp (30 mL) amaranth seeds

1 Tbsp (15 mL) buckwheat groats

1 Tbsp (15 mL) teff grains

2 Tbsp (30 mL) raisins

1 tsp (5 mL) chia seeds

Pinch of cinnamon

1 cup (250 mL) boiling water

2 Tbsp (30 mL) milk (optional)

1 Tbsp (15 mL) nuts, your choice (optional)

WALNUT, ORANGE & DATE KAÑIWA BREAKFAST CEREAL

SERVES 2

Don't settle for boring! Sweet orange, dates and walnuts combine with kañiwa to make this fragrant, tasty and invigorating breakfast cereal.

1½ cups (375 mL) water

¾ cup (175 mL) kañiwa

⅓ cup (75 mL) freshly squeezed orange juice

¼ cup (60 mL) chopped dates

¼ tsp (1 mL) cinnamon

1 tsp (5 mL) honey (optional)

2 Tbsp (30 mL) finely chopped walnuts

Brown sugar (optional)

Milk (optional)

Combine the water and kañiwa in a small saucepan and bring to a boil. Cover, reduce to a simmer and cook for 15 minutes. Remove the lid. Stir in the orange juice, dates and cinnamon, continuing to simmer, uncovered, until the liquid has reduced. Stir in the honey, if using. Divide between two bowls and serve with walnuts, brown sugar and milk if desired.

PER SERVING: Energy 430 calories; Protein 16 g; Carbohydrates 69 g; Dietary Fiber 7 g; Fat 11 g; Sugar 18 g; Cholesterol 0 mg; Sodium 10 mg.

- Want more orange flavor? Add a pinch of orange zest. See how to preserve your own orange zest on page 71.
- For a change, try making this recipe with 2 cups (500 mL) of cooked millet, quinoa, sorghum, buckwheat, steel-cut oats or cooked and rinsed amaranth or teff.

CREAMY SLOW-COOKED STEEL-CUT OATS

SERVES 4

Move over, oat flakes—steel-cut oats are here to stay! Chunky and chewy, steel-cut oats have an impressive, wholesome texture that is filling and satisfying. Make your morning awesome with a hot bowl of comforting and creamy steel-cut oats. This recipe will fit into your busy schedule since it only takes 5 minutes to put in your 4-quart (4 L) slow cooker the night before. Serve topped with your choice of fruit, nuts, sweetener and milk.

Place oats, water, milk, vanilla and salt (if using) in slow cooker and stir. Cook on low, covered, for 6 to 8 hours. Stir and serve with desired toppings.

PER SERVING: Energy 270 calories; Protein 13 g; Carbohydrates 47 g; Dietary Fiber 6 g; Fat 5 g; Sugar 6 g; Cholesterol 5 mg; Sodium 60 mg.

1½ cups (375 mL) steel-cut oats
4 cups (1 L) water
2 cups (500 mL) 1% milk, milk substitute or light coconut milk
1½ tsp (7 mL) pure vanilla extract
Pinch of salt (optional)

> If adding dried fruit to the cereal, do so at the beginning or end of the cooking process, depending on whether you prefer it well hydrated. Nuts can be added just before serving.

PUMPKIN SPICE STEEL-CUT OATS

SERVES 6

Serve a unique hot breakfast to satisfy everyone's early morning hunger. Spicy pumpkin flavors in a breakfast cereal will have family and friends wondering where you found the time. This super simple recipe is just thrown together before bed and it will be ready and cooked to perfection by the time you wake up.

1½ cups (375 mL) steel-cut oats

2 cups (500 mL) 1% milk

4 cups (1 L) water

1 cup (250 mL) pumpkin purée

1½ tsp (7 mL) cinnamon

½ tsp (2 mL) ground ginger

¼ tsp (1 mL) nutmeg

1 Tbsp (15 mL) pure vanilla extract

⅓ cup (75 mL) pure maple syrup
    or brown sugar

Pumpkin seeds (optional)

Vanilla yogurt, cream, milk or ice
    cream (optional)

Place the oats, milk, water, pumpkin, cinnamon, ginger and nutmeg in slow cooker. Cook on low for 7 to 8 hours. Stir in the vanilla and maple syrup. Serve with pumpkin seeds, yogurt, cream, milk or ice cream if desired.

PER SERVING: Energy 240 calories; Protein 9 g; Carbohydrates 46 g; Dietary Fiber 5 g; Fat 3.5 g; Sugar 16 g; Cholesterol 5 mg; Sodium 45 mg.

> Does the size of your slow cooker matter? Yes. Using a slow cooker that is larger than required may result in overcooked food.

LEMON CASHEW GINGER ANCIENT GRAIN GRANOLA

MAKES 3¹/2 CUPS (875 ML), 7 SERVINGS

If you're currently buying expensive gourmet granola, or wishing that you could, now you can make your own. Lemon, cashews, ginger, coconut and dried pineapple make this a seriously gourmet breakfast treat.

4 tsp (20 mL) fresh lemon zest

¼ cup (60 mL) quinoa seeds

1½ Tbsp (22 mL) teff grains

1½ Tbsp (22 mL) amaranth seeds

1¼ cups (300 mL) large-flake rolled oats

½ cup (125 mL) unsweetened shredded coconut

2 Tbsp (30 mL) chia seeds

⅓ cup (75 mL) roasted salted cashews (or plain raw cashews)

½ cup (125 mL) honey or pure maple syrup

½ tsp (2 mL) cinnamon

½ tsp (2 mL) ground ginger

1 tsp (5 mL) pure vanilla extract

⅓ cup (75 mL) diced dried pineapple or mango

Preheat the oven to 200°F (100°C). Lay zest evenly without any clumps on a baking sheet lined with parchment or a silicone mat and place in the oven. Immediately turn the heat off and leave zest in the oven for 7 to 9 minutes. Remove the baking sheet and place the zest in a small bowl. Set aside.

Preheat the oven to 275°F (140°C) and line one large or two small baking sheets with parchment or a silicone mat.

Place the quinoa, teff and amaranth in a sealable plastic bag. Roll gently with a rolling pin to crack the exterior of the seeds for optimal nutrient absorption. Place the cracked grains, oats, coconut, chia and cashews in a large bowl.

In a small bowl, whisk together the honey, cinnamon, ginger and vanilla. Pour over the grains and stir until completely coated. Spread evenly on the prepared baking sheet(s) and bake for 15 minutes. Stir and bake for another 15 minutes. Remove from the oven and cool until manageable. Pour into a large bowl and stir in the dried pineapple and lemon zest. Allow granola to cool and dry out before placing in a sealable container for up to 3 months. Serve on thick plain Greek yogurt and honey (if desired) or with milk.

PER SERVING: Energy 200 calories; Protein 4 g; Carbohydrates 33 g; Dietary Fiber 3 g; Fat 6 g; Sugar 17 g; Cholesterol 0 mg; Sodium 5 mg.

APPLE RAISIN SPICE GRANOLA

MAKES 5 CUPS (1.25 L), 10 SERVINGS

Soft raisins and apples are tossed in a lightly sweetened, toasted and spiced combination of ancient grains and seeds. Have satisfaction knowing you made this great granola yourself.

Preheat the oven to 225°F (110°C) and place a rack in the center. Place a piece of parchment on the bottom of a large baking sheet. Place the quinoa, teff and amaranth in a sealable plastic bag and roll with a rolling pin to gently crack.

In a large bowl, combine the cracked grains with oats, buckwheat, pumpkin seeds and sunflower seeds. In a small bowl or measuring cup, whisk together the maple syrup and vanilla until thoroughly mixed. Pour syrup mixture over the oat mixture and stir until evenly coated. Sprinkle with chia seeds, cinnamon and nutmeg. Stir until spices have evenly coated the mixture.

Pour evenly on the prepared baking sheet. Bake in the preheated oven for 1 hour, stirring every 20 minutes. Remove from the oven and cool completely. Stir in the raisins and apples. Store granola in a sealable container.

PER SERVING: Energy 310 calories; Protein 9 g; Carbohydrates 49 g; Dietary Fiber 6 g; Fat 9 g; Sugar 17 g; Cholesterol 0 mg; Sodium 20 mg.

½ cup (125 mL) quinoa seeds
2 Tbsp (30 mL) teff grains
2 Tbsp (30 mL) amaranth seeds
2 cups (500 mL) large-flake
   rolled oats
½ cup (125 mL) buckwheat groats
½ cup (125 mL) raw unsalted
   pumpkin seeds
¼ cup (60 mL) unsalted
   sunflower seeds
½ cup (125 mL) pure maple syrup
   or honey
1 tsp (5 mL) pure vanilla extract
¼ cup (60 mL) chia seeds
2 tsp (10 mL) cinnamon
Pinch of nutmeg
½ cup (125 mL) raisins
½ cup (125 mL) diced dried apple

- Instead of quinoa, try millet.
- Make any of the granola recipes into muesli by omitting the honey mixture and spices. Toast for 15 minutes to enhance the flavor if desired, but this step is not necessary.

CHEWY CHOCOLATE GRANOLA WITH CHERRIES & BUCKWHEAT

MAKES 5 CUPS (1.25 L), 10 SERVINGS

Make your own granola cheaper and even tastier than you can buy it. This delicious granola can be made chewy or crunchy—you choose. Use cherries, cranberries, or for something a little different, try a combination of your favorite chopped nuts.

1 cup (250 mL) quick-cooking
    oats (not instant)
1 cup (250 mL) quinoa flakes
¾ cup (175 mL) buckwheat groats
½ cup (125 mL) flaked
    unsweetened coconut
½ cup (125 mL) slivered almonds
¾ cup (175 mL) honey
3 Tbsp (45 mL) grapeseed oil
3 Tbsp (45 mL) unsweetened
    cocoa powder
Pinch of salt
¼ tsp (1 mL) baking soda
1½ tsp (7 mL) pure vanilla extract
½ cup (125 mL) dried cherries

Preheat the oven to 275°F (140°C) and line a large rimmed baking sheet (21 × 15 inches/52 × 38 cm) with parchment or a silicone mat. Set aside.

In a large bowl, stir together the oats, quinoa flakes, buckwheat, coconut and almonds.

In a small saucepan, combine the honey, oil, cocoa and salt. Heat on medium-low, stirring frequently. When it has bubbled for 1 minute, stir in the baking soda and vanilla. Remove from the heat and pour over the oat mixture. Stir until evenly coated. Using a spatula, scrape the mixture onto the prepared baking sheet, flatten into an even layer not more than ½ inch (1 cm) thick and bake for 10 minutes for chewy granola or 20 minutes for crunchy granola. Remove from the heat and allow to cool enough to manage. Pour into a large clean bowl and toss with the cherries. Store in a sealable container for up to 1 month.

PER SERVING (½ cup/125 mL): Energy 310 calories; Protein 6 g; Carbohydrates 52 g; Dietary Fiber 6 g; Fat 11 g; Sugar 23 g; Cholesterol 0 mg; Sodium 170 mg.

Alternatively, replace the quinoa flakes with an equal amount of millet, amaranth or buckwheat flakes.

MOLASSES SPICE GRANOLA WITH PUMPKIN SEEDS & CRANBERRIES

MAKES 4¹/₂ CUPS (1.1 L), 9 SERVINGS

This lightly spiced granola has the crunch of pumpkin seeds and tart-sweet cranberries for a delightful blend of flavors. Enjoy with yogurt, milk or as a snack on the go.

Preheat the oven to 225°F (110°C). Place a piece of parchment on a large baking sheet.

In a large bowl, combine the oats, buckwheat, pumpkin seeds, millet, sunflower seeds, teff and amaranth; set aside. In a small bowl or measuring cup, whisk together the maple syrup, molasses and vanilla extract until well blended. Pour the molasses mixture over the oat mixture and stir until evenly coated. Sprinkle with chia seeds, cinnamon, ginger and nutmeg. Stir until spices are evenly distributed.

Pour evenly on the prepared baking sheet. Bake in the preheated oven for 1 hour, stirring every 20 minutes. Remove from the oven and cool completely. Stir in the cranberries and store in a sealable container.

PER SERVING: Energy 330 calories; Protein 10 g; Carbohydrates 53 g; Dietary Fiber 7 g; Fat 10 g; Sugar 18 g; Cholesterol 0 mg; Sodium 5 mg.

> Try kasha (roasted buckwheat) instead of buckwheat groats, quinoa instead of millet and sesame seeds instead of sunflower seeds.

2 cups (500 mL) large-flake rolled oats
½ cup (125 mL) buckwheat groats
½ cup (125 mL) raw unsalted pumpkin seeds
½ cup (125 mL) millet seeds
¼ cup (60 mL) unsalted sunflower seeds
2 Tbsp (30 mL) teff grains
2 Tbsp (30 mL) amaranth seeds
½ cup (125 mL) pure maple syrup or honey
2 tsp (10 mL) fancy molasses
1 tsp (5 mL) pure vanilla extract
3 Tbsp (45 mL) chia seeds
2 tsp (10 mL) cinnamon
Pinch of ground ginger
Pinch of nutmeg
½ cup (125 mL) sweetened (or unsweetened) dried cranberries

Chewy Chocolate Granola
with Cherries & Buckwheat

BUCKWHEAT CRÊPES

MAKES 10 CRÊPES

Buckwheat crêpes are a wonderfully flavorful alternative to plain crêpes and are just as simple. Enjoy them with any of your favorite toppings for breakfast or dessert. Make these crêpes for the Caramel Apple Buckwheat Crêpes recipe (page 166). These crêpes can be made 1 day ahead of time.

⅔ cups (175 mL) buckwheat flour
2 tsp (10 mL) cornstarch
2 large eggs
2 egg whites
1 cup (250 mL) 1% milk
1 Tbsp (15 mL) pure maple syrup
Pinch of salt

Whisk the flour and cornstarch in a medium bowl. Add the eggs, egg whites, milk, maple syrup and salt. Whisk batter until combined and smooth.

Preheat a lightly oiled 6-inch (15 cm) crêpe pan or skillet on medium-high heat. Pour 3 Tbsp (45 mL) batter into the center of the pan and tilt pan to move the batter in a circular motion to make a round crêpe. Flip crêpe when the edges begin to curl (about 30 to 45 seconds). Cook the other side of crêpe for another 30 seconds, place on a plate and cover with foil. Repeat steps with remaining batter. Enjoy with your favorite toppings.

PER SERVING (per crêpe): Energy 60 calories; Protein 4 g; Carbohydrates 9 g; Dietary Fiber 1 g; Fat 1.5 g; Sugar 3 g; Cholesterol 40 mg; Sodium 65 mg.

OAT & SORGHUM BLUEBERRY BUTTERMILK GRIDDLE CAKES

MAKES 12 PANCAKES, 4 SERVINGS

Easily the perfect pancake, these look like they're fresh out of grandma's farmhouse kitchen. These pancakes are golden, fluffy and sturdy and they taste delicious! Omega-3-rich chia gel replaces the oil in the batter. Seriously scrumptious!

Combine chia and boiling water in a small bowl. Gently stir with a fork to ensure the ground seeds are evenly distributed. Set aside to thicken.

Preheat the oven to 200°F (100°C). In a medium bowl, combine the oat flour, sorghum flour, baking powder, baking soda and salt; mix until well combined. Set aside.

In another small bowl, whisk together egg, buttermilk, chia mixture and vanilla. Add the buttermilk mixture to the flour mixture and stir until just combined. Do not overmix.

Preheat a skillet on medium heat. Brush with butter or grapeseed oil. Use a ¼-cup (60 mL) measure to scoop batter onto skillet. Gently press 6 to 8 blueberries onto each pancake. Flip pancakes when batter begins to bubble, approximately 3 minutes per side. Bottom should be golden. Pancakes are done if they spring back when gently pressed. Keep warm in a covered ovenproof baking dish in the preheated oven until remaining pancakes are done. Serve with syrup, yogurt or fruit toppings.

2 tsp (10 mL) ground chia seeds
3 Tbsp (45 mL) boiling water
½ cup (125 mL) oat flour
½ cup (125 mL) sorghum flour
¼ tsp (1 mL) baking powder
¾ tsp (3 mL) baking soda
¼ tsp (1 mL) salt
1 large egg, beaten
1 cup (250 mL) buttermilk
1 tsp (5 mL) pure vanilla extract
1 cup (250 mL) fresh blueberries

PER SERVING: Energy 170 calories; Protein 8 g; Carbohydrates 28 g; Dietary Fiber 4 g; Fat 3.5 g; Sugar 7 g; Cholesterol 50 mg; Sodium 400 mg.

CHOCOLATE TEFF WAFFLES

SERVES 6

A decadent-looking dark cocoa waffle ready for all your favorite toppings. Chocolate with the nutrition of protein-rich teff that even contains a dose of vitamin C also makes a great dessert, warmed and topped with fruit, chocolate sauce or whipped cream. Or why not try it topped with our Raspberry Chia Jam (page 35)?

2 cups (500 mL) teff flour

¼ cup (60 mL) unsweetened cocoa powder

4 tsp (20 mL) baking powder

¼ cup (60 mL) white or organic cane sugar

½ tsp (2 mL) salt

2 large eggs

1¼ cups (300 mL) 1% or 2% milk

1 cup (250 mL) water

½ cup (125 mL) vegetable oil

2 tsp (10 mL) pure vanilla extract

Preheat the oven to 200°F (100°C). Combine teff flour, cocoa, baking powder, sugar, and salt in a large bowl and set aside. In a medium bowl, beat eggs, then stir in milk, water, oil and vanilla. Add wet ingredients to dry, making a thin batter. Ladle batter into a greased preheated waffle iron. Remove waffles when lid lifts easily, approximately 5 to 6 minutes. Keep warm in a covered ovenproof baking dish in the preheated oven until remaining waffles are done. Waffles will keep in the refrigerator for up to 3 days and can be reheated in a toaster.

PER SERVING: Energy 400 calories; Protein 10 g; Carbohydrates 42 g; Dietary Fiber 7 g; Fat 21 g; Sugar 11 g; Cholesterol 65 mg; Sodium 250 mg.

Possible waffle toppings include yogurt, maple syrup, fruit syrup, peanut butter, sliced bananas, pineapple, berries or other fresh fruit.

CINNAMON RAISIN SCONES

MAKES 10 SCONES

The buttery cinnamon combination of a deliciously warm cinnamon roll in a gluten-free scone. Plump raisins and a sprinkle of brown sugar on top kick these sorghum and oat scones up a notch.

Combine chia and boiling water in a small bowl. Gently stir with a fork to ensure ground seeds are evenly distributed and set aside to thicken. Lightly grease or line a baking sheet with parchment. Preheat the oven to 400°F (200°C).

In a large bowl, combine the sorghum flour, oat flour, baking powder, xanthan gum, cane sugar, cinnamon and salt. Cut in ¼ cup (60 mL) butter using a pastry blender, two knives or your fingers, pinching butter into pea-sized lumps. Stir in raisins. Mix together buttermilk, chia mixture and yogurt. Add buttermilk mixture to the flour mixture and stir gently until just combined. Do not overmix.

Using floured hands, pat dough into 2½-inch (7.5 cm) balls and place on prepared baking sheet. Flatten slightly. Melt 1 Tbsp (15 mL) butter in a small saucepan; stir in brown sugar. Spoon approximately ¾ tsp (3 mL) of mixture on top of each scone.

Bake on the center rack for 15 minutes. Remove from the oven and serve warm.

1 tsp (5 mL) ground chia seeds

1½ Tbsp (22 mL) boiling water

1 cup (250 mL) sorghum flour

¾ cup (175 mL) oat flour

4 tsp (20 mL) baking powder

1 tsp (5 mL) xanthan gum

3 Tbsp (45 mL) white or
    organic cane sugar

½ tsp (2 mL) cinnamon

Pinch of salt

¼ cup (60 mL) cold
    unsalted butter

¾ cup (175 mL) raisins

½ cup (125 mL) low-fat buttermilk

¼ cup (60 mL) plain low-fat yogurt

1 Tbsp (15 mL) unsalted butter

2 Tbsp (30 mL) brown sugar

PER SERVING: Energy 190 calories; Protein 4 g; Carbohydrates 30 g; Dietary Fiber 3 g; Fat 7 g; Sugar 13 g; Cholesterol 15 mg; Sodium 50 mg.

WHITE CHOCOLATE RASPBERRY SORGHUM & OAT SCONES

MAKES 9 SCONES (3 INCHES/8 CM WIDE)

For a hit combination, these scones are gently sweetened with white chocolate and full of tangy raspberry taste.

Preheat the oven to 400°F (200°C) with the oven rack in the center position. Place a piece of parchment or silicone mat on a large baking sheet and set aside.

In a medium bowl, whisk together the sorghum flour, oat flour, potato starch, baking powder, xanthan gum and salt. Cut in the cold butter with a pastry blender until the butter is pea-sized. Gently fold in the raspberries and set aside.

Whisk the egg, then stir in the buttermilk, brown sugar and vanilla. Gently fold the egg mixture into the flour mixture until just moistened. Scoop the dough with a ¼-cup (60 mL) measure and place at least 2 inches (5 cm) apart on the prepared baking sheet. Dust your hands with a little potato starch and gently pat and form into 2½-inch (6 cm) wide and ¾-inch (2 cm) thick rounds.

Bake for 10 to 12 minutes or until the edges and bottom are golden. Remove from the oven and cool slightly. Melt the chocolate in either a double boiler or the microwave (stirring every 15 seconds until melted). Drizzle with a spoon or pour into a sealable plastic bag, cut a ¼-inch (5 mm) tip in the corner and draw diagonal lines across each scone. Serve immediately.

½ cup (125 mL) sorghum flour
½ cup (125 mL) oat flour
⅓ cup (75 mL) potato starch (with a little extra for hands)
2 tsp (10 mL) baking powder
1½ tsp (7 mL) xanthan gum
¼ tsp (1 mL) salt
⅓ cup (75 mL) cold unsalted butter
¾ cup (175 mL) fresh raspberries
1 large egg
¼ cup (60 mL) buttermilk
3 Tbsp (45 mL) brown sugar
¾ tsp (3 mL) pure vanilla extract
¼ cup (60 mL) white chocolate chips

PER SERVING: Energy 260 calories; Protein 4 g; Carbohydrates 31 g; Dietary Fiber 3 g; Fat 14 g; Sugar 9 g; Cholesterol 60 mg; Sodium 125 mg.

- Substitute semi-sweet chocolate for white chocolate if you prefer.
- Wild blueberries may replace the raspberries in this recipe.
- Large raspberries can be frozen in a single layer, then chopped into smaller pieces and added still frozen.

TOASTED COCONUT FRUIT SALAD WITH QUINOA & PINEAPPLE LIME DRESSING

SERVES 4

Easy and so tasty! This is a great option for breakfast, brunch, lunch or an anytime healthy snack. Full of the light, fruity flavor of pineapple and coconut, this salad is a must-have for family gatherings.

1⅓ cups (300 mL) water

⅔ cup (150 mL) quinoa seeds

¼ to ⅓ cup (60 to 75 mL) unsweetened dried coconut

3 ripe kiwis, peeled, quartered and each quarter cut into thirds

1 cup (250 mL) diced strawberries

1 can (14 oz/398 mL) pineapple tidbits, drained, ⅓ cup (75 mL) juice reserved

1 Tbsp (15 mL) freshly squeezed lime juice (about 1 lime)

Combine the water and quinoa in a medium saucepan. Bring to a boil, reduce to a simmer and cook with the cover on for 15 minutes. Remove from the heat and set aside with the cover off to cool completely.

Preheat a sauté pan on medium heat. Add coconut. Stir constantly until it turns a golden color and is fragrant (about 1 to 3 minutes). Remove from the heat and set aside to cool.

In a medium bowl, toss the quinoa, kiwi, strawberries and pineapple with the reserved pineapple juice and lime juice. Sprinkle with coconut just prior to serving.

PER SERVING: Energy 220 calories; Protein 6 g; Carbohydrates 39 g; Dietary Fiber 6 g; Fat 5 g; Sugar 15 g; Cholesterol 0 mg; Sodium 10 mg.

- As an alternative, add ½ cup (125 mL) fresh blueberries, blackberries or pomegranate seeds.
- Add honey or maple syrup for added sweetness.
- No quinoa or want to a change it up? Use 2 cups (500 mL) cooked sorghum.

PROSCIUTTO & KALE KAÑIWA FRITTATA WITH ROMANO CHEESE

SERVES 4

Vegetables for breakfast? Absolutely! A good dose of the nutrient-rich superfood kale completes this kañiwa frittata that also gets a bold hit of personality from salty prosciutto. Also share this for lunch or supper.

In a small saucepan, combine the water and kañiwa and bring to a boil. Reduce to a simmer, cover and cook for 15 minutes. Remove from the heat, drain if necessary, fluff with a fork and set aside to cool.

Preheat a 10-inch (25 cm) nonstick ovenproof skillet on medium heat and add the oil. Cook the kale and prosciutto until the kale is tender (about 4 minutes). Remove from the heat.

Meanwhile, whisk the cooled kañiwa with the eggs, egg whites, milk, basil, salt (if using) and pepper. Reheat the kale and prosciutto to medium and preheat the broiler. Pour egg mixture over the kale and prosciutto in the skillet. Cook the mixture gently, stirring and lifting the eggs from the sides. Sprinkle the eggs with green onion and cheese when the eggs start to set. Place the skillet under the broiler for a few minutes to finish cooking the egg and melting the cheese. Cut into servings and enjoy.

PER SERVING: Energy 280 calories; Protein 21 g; Carbohydrates 13 g; Dietary Fiber 2 g; Fat 17 g; Sugar 2 g; Cholesterol 165 mg; Sodium 870 mg.

½ cup (125 mL) water
¼ cup (60 mL) kañiwa seeds
2 Tbsp (30 mL) grapeseed or vegetable oil
1½ cups (375 mL) thinly sliced kale, ribs removed
3 oz (85 g) prosciutto, cut into 1-inch (2.5 cm) square pieces
3 large eggs
4 large egg whites
¼ cup (60 mL) skim milk
1 Tbsp (15 mL) chopped fresh basil
½ tsp (2 mL) salt (optional)
Pinch of freshly ground pepper
¼ cup (60 mL) thinly sliced green onion
⅓ to ½ cup (75 to 125 mL) freshly grated Romano or Parmesan cheese

- For a totally different frittata, you can substitute quinoa, millet or amaranth for the kañiwa.
- Kale not available? Use an equal amount of baby spinach instead.

APPETIZERS, SNACKS, SALADS & SIDE DISHES

Back to nature! Easy and packed with whole-food goodness, ancient grains have both practical and creative uses in so many different dishes. Whether it's simple snacks, impressing guests with fancy finger foods, or salads for side dishes and lunch boxes, ancient grains do the trick.

Looking for easy family snacks or attractive appetizers? Try any of the homemade cracker recipes, such as Cheddar Thyme Quinoa Crackers with Sea Salt, Six Seed & Onion Quinoa Crackers or Toasted Sesame Quinoa Crackers on pages 74–80. Rustic artisan crackers are splendid for showing off to guests, especially with the Basil & White Bean Amaranth Dip (page 83) or Red Pepper Chipotle Superblend Hummus (page 83). Need a speedy side dish for tonight's dinner? Try the Cucumber Cashew Quinoa & Buckwheat Salad with Mint (page 87). Or if you need to make something ahead for a week's worth of lunches, try Fresh Corn & Millet Bean Salad with Thyme Vinaigrette (page 88) or Asparagus & Sweet Baby Pea Quinoa Pilaf with Parmesan Cheese (page 98).

CHILI LIME POPPED AMARANTH

....

MAKES 1 CUP (250 ML), 2 SERVINGS

The spicy chili and lime combination makes this popped amaranth (or sorghum) a tasty topping for salads, soup or eggs or just eating on its own. Keeps in an airtight container for up to 1 month.

1 tsp (5 mL) freshly grated lime zest

4 Tbsp (60 mL) amaranth seeds

1 Tbsp (15 mL) unsalted butter, melted

¼ to ½ tsp (1 to 2 mL) chili powder or ¼ tsp (1 mL) ground chipotle pepper

¼ tsp (1 mL) salt

¼ tsp (1 mL) garlic powder (optional)

Preheat the oven to 200°F (100°C). Line a baking sheet with parchment or a silicone mat and arrange zest thinly in a single layer and place in the oven. Turn the oven off and remove the baking sheet after 7 to 9 minutes.

Heat a dry 10- or 12-inch (25 or 30 cm) sauté pan with lid over medium heat for at least 1½ minutes. Place 1 Tbsp (15 mL) amaranth in the pan and cover quickly. Move pan from side to side on the burner. The seeds should start popping immediately. Remove pan from the heat when you can see that three-quarters of the amaranth has popped or when the popping has begun to reduce. Keep lid on to pop any remaining seeds. Repeat with remaining 3 Tbsp (45 mL) amaranth. Place popped amaranth in a bowl and toss in the butter, chili powder, salt, zest and garlic powder (if using). Set aside to cool and dry completely.

NOTE: As each stove heats differently and each type of pan conducts heat differently, it may take longer than 1½ minutes to reach optimum popping temperature. Also, it may take more than one try to know how your timing and temperature work.

PER SERVING: Energy 140 calories; Protein 3 g; Carbohydrates 16 g; Dietary Fiber 2 g; Fat 7 g; Sugar 0 g; Cholesterol 15 mg; Sodium 300 mg.

- Zest it up! Don't waste another citrus rind—dry the zest of lemons, limes, oranges and grapefruits. With a fine grater, zest only the top colored layer of the fruit and not the pith or white bitter layer underneath. Preheat the oven to 200°F (100°C). Lay zest thinly without clumps on a baking sheet lined with parchment or a silicone mat and place in the oven. Turn the oven off and remove the baking sheet after 7 to 9 minutes. Another option would be to place zest on a tray or plate and allow to completely dry, for approximately 4 hours. 1½ to 2 tsp (7 to 10 mL) of fresh zest makes about 1 tsp (5 mL) dried zest. Store it in airtight containers. Use it in any of your favorite recipes, such as icing, baking, drinks or granolas, or on steamed vegetables. The flavor is best for about 2 weeks but can last longer if frozen. You can also use the dried zest in the Curry & Orange Popped Amaranth (page 72) or the Lemon, Thyme & Garlic Popped Amaranth (page 73).
- Instead of amaranth, try using sorghum grains.

CURRY & ORANGE POPPED AMARANTH

....

MAKES 1 CUP (250 ML), 2 SERVINGS

A hint of curry spice and lively orange make this popped amaranth or sorghum a unique, impressive and tasty topping for salad or soup or just eating on its own. Keeps in an airtight container for up to 1 month.

1 tsp (5 mL) freshly grated
   orange zest
4 Tbsp (60 mL) amaranth seeds
1 Tbsp (15 mL) unsalted butter,
   melted
¼ to ½ tsp (1 to 2 mL) curry
   powder
¼ tsp (1 mL) salt

Preheat the oven to 200°F (100°C). Line a baking sheet with parchment or a silicone mat and arrange zest thinly in a single layer; place in the oven. Turn the oven off and remove the baking sheet after 7 to 9 minutes.

Heat a dry 10- or 12-inch (25 or 30 cm) sauté pan with lid over medium heat for at least 1½ minutes. Place 1 Tbsp (15 mL) amaranth in the pan and cover quickly. Move pan from side to side on the burner. The seeds should start popping immediately. Remove pan from the heat when you can see that three-quarters of the amaranth has popped or when the popping begins to reduce. Keep lid on to pop any remaining seeds. Repeat with remaining 3 Tbsp (45 mL) amaranth. Place popped amaranth in a bowl and toss in the butter, curry power, zest and salt. Set aside to cool and dry completely.

PER SERVING: Energy 140 calories; Protein 3 g; Carbohydrates 16 g; Dietary Fiber 2 g; Fat 8 g; Sugar 0 g; Cholesterol 15 mg; Sodium 240 mg.

Instead of amaranth, try using sorghum grains.

LEMON, THYME & GARLIC POPPED AMARANTH

MAKES 1 CUP (250 ML), 2 SERVINGS

Thyme, zesty lemon and buttery garlic makes this popped amaranth or sorghum a warm and familiar addition to soups, salads and appetizers.

Preheat the oven to 200°F (100°C). Line a baking sheet with parchment or a silicone mat and arrange zest thinly in a single layer; place in the oven. Turn the oven off and remove the baking sheet after 7 to 9 minutes.

Heat a dry 10- or 12-inch (25 or 30 cm) sauté pan with lid over medium heat for at least 1½ minutes. Place 1 Tbsp (15 mL) amaranth in the pan and cover quickly. Move pan from side to side on the burner. The seeds should start popping immediately. Remove pan from the heat when you can see that three-quarters of the amaranth has popped or when the popping begins to slow. Keep lid on to pop any remaining seeds. Repeat with remaining 3 Tbsp (45 mL) amaranth. Place popped seeds in a bowl and toss in the butter, thyme, garlic powder, zest and salt. Set aside to cool and dry completely.

1 tsp (5 mL) freshly grated
   lemon zest
4 Tbsp (60 mL) amaranth seeds
1 Tbsp (15 mL) unsalted butter,
   melted
¼ to ½ tsp (1 to 2 mL) dried thyme
¼ to ½ tsp (1 to 2 mL) garlic
   powder
¼ tsp (1 mL) salt

PER SERVING: Energy 140 calories; Protein 3 g; Carbohydrates 16 g; Dietary Fiber 2 g; Fat 7 g; Sugar 0 g; Cholesterol 15 mg; Sodium 240 mg.

Instead of amaranth, try using sorghum grains.

Amaranth seeds

CHEDDAR THYME QUINOA CRACKERS WITH SEA SALT

MAKES 40 CRACKERS

The luxury of a homemade artisan cracker with a fresh burst of herb and cheese flavor. Pair this cracker with your favorite dip, such as the Red Pepper Chipotle Superblend Hummus (page 83), or toppings, or serve with additional appetizers, cheese and crudités.

1 cup (250 mL) quinoa flakes

⅓ cup (75 mL) shredded aged Cheddar or Gouda cheese

1½ tsp (7 mL) chopped fresh thyme or ½ tsp (2 mL) dried thyme

Pinch of ground chipotle or cayenne pepper (optional)

⅓ cup (75 mL) hot water

1½ tsp (7 mL) liquid honey

3 Tbsp (45 mL) white rice or potato flour for rolling

¼ tsp (1 mL) sea salt

> Try a variation with an equal amount of millet or amaranth flakes.

Preheat the oven to 325°F (160°C) with the oven rack in the center. Cut two pieces of parchment the same size as a large baking sheet.

Combine the quinoa flakes, cheese, thyme and chipotle pepper (if using) in a medium bowl. Stir until ingredients are evenly dispersed. Pour in the hot water and honey. Use your hands to mix into a ball (the dough should not be too sticky but should hold well together). Flatten ball into a disk. If edges begin to crack, add a bit more water. If the dough is too sticky, add more quinoa flakes.

Place the disk (or divide into two disks, if they're easier to handle) between the pieces of parchment, dust with flour and roll $\frac{1}{16}$ inch (1.5 mm) thick. For a thicker cracker, ⅛ inch (3 mm) is acceptable but will need to be baked longer. Check frequently to ensure dough is not sticking; redust with flour if necessary. Peel away the top piece of parchment and place bottom parchment and dough on the baking sheet. Sprinkle with sea salt. Cut crackers with a 2-inch (5 cm) round cookie cutter, leaving crackers within the cut dough. Bake in the preheated oven for 10 minutes. Remove the baking sheet from the oven. Place the second piece of parchment on top of the cracker dough and flip. Place the bottom parchment and crackers on the baking sheet (it is fine if crackers separate) and bake for another 7 to 10 minutes, depending on the thickness of your cracker. Watch closely in the last 5 minutes to prevent burning. Remove any crackers on the edges of the parchment that are getting too browned. Crackers should be fairly dry and slightly golden when done. Remove from the oven to cool and dry completely (to get crispy), especially if they are slightly chewy. Store crackers in a sealable container.

PER SERVING (4 crackers): Energy 50 calories; Protein 3 g; Carbohydrates 10 g; Dietary Fiber 1 g; Fat 1 g; Sugar 1 g; Cholesterol 0 mg; Sodium 150 mg.

SIX SEED & ONION QUINOA CRACKERS

MAKES 60 CRACKERS

A beautiful and hardy combination of seeds and grains makes these delicious and nutritious crackers look like art. Serve with an array of fruit and cheeses (especially aged Cheddar) for a savory snack.

Preheat the oven to 325°F (160°C), place the oven rack in center position and cut two pieces of parchment to fit a large baking sheet.

Combine the quinoa flakes, sunflower seeds, sesame seeds, poppy seeds, chia seeds, teff, amaranth and onion salt in a medium bowl. Stir until ingredients are evenly combined. Pour in the hot water. Use your hands to mix into a ball (the dough should not be too sticky but should hold well together). Flatten ball into a disk. If edges begin to crack, add a bit more water. If the dough is too sticky, add more quinoa flakes.

Place the disk (or divide into two disks, if easier) between the two pieces of parchment, dust with flour and roll 1⁄16 inch (1.5 mm) thick. For a thicker cracker, 1⁄8 inch (3 mm) is acceptable but will need to be baked longer. Peel away the top parchment and place dough and bottom parchment on the baking sheet. Sprinkle with sea salt (if using). Bake in preheated oven for 10 minutes. Remove the baking sheet from the oven. Place the second piece of parchment on top of the cracker dough again. Flip dough over between the pieces of parchment.

Remove the top parchment and cut into 1¼-inch (3 cm) squares with a pizza wheel or knife. Place the bottom parchment and crackers on the baking sheet (if crackers separate, that is fine) and bake for another 7 to 10 minutes, depending on the thickness of the cracker. Watch closely in the last 5 minutes to prevent burning. Remove any crackers on the edges of the parchment that are getting too browned. Crackers should be fairly dry and slightly golden. Remove from the oven to cool and dry completely (to get crispy), especially if they are slightly chewy. Store crackers in a sealable container.

PER SERVING (4 crackers): Energy 45 calories; Protein 2 g; Carbohydrates 7 g; Dietary Fiber 1 g; Fat 1.5 g; Sugar 0 g; Cholesterol 0 mg; Sodium 250 mg.

1 cup (250 mL) quinoa flakes
2 Tbsp (30 mL) sunflower seeds
1 Tbsp (15 mL) sesame seeds
1½ tsp (7 mL) poppy seeds
1½ tsp (7 mL) chia seeds
1½ tsp (7 mL) teff grains
1½ tsp (7 ml) amaranth seeds
1½ tsp (7 mL) onion salt
1⁄3 cup (75 mL) hot water
3 Tbsp (45 mL) white rice or
     potato flour for rolling
¼ tsp (1 mL) sea salt (optional)

Use millet or amaranth flakes in place of quinoa for a different-flavored cracker.

TOASTED SESAME QUINOA CRACKERS

MAKES 25 CRACKERS

A familiar sesame cracker gets a gluten-free makeover with a nutritious dose of healthy quinoa, as well as a splash of sweet and salty with honey and sea salt. Make a statement by serving these long crackers alongside an Asian soup, stir-fry, savory soup or stew.

1 cup (250 mL) quinoa flakes
3 Tbsp (45 mL) sesame seeds
1 Tbsp (15 mL) toasted sesame oil
⅓ cup (75 mL) hot water
1 Tbsp (15 mL) liquid honey
3 Tbsp (45 mL) white rice or
   potato flour for rolling
¼ tsp (1 mL) sea salt

Try an equal amount of millet or amaranth flakes in place of quinoa flakes.

Preheat the oven to 325°F (160°C) with oven rack in center position. Cut two pieces of parchment that will fit a large baking sheet.

Combine the quinoa flakes, sesame seeds and sesame oil in a medium bowl. Stir until ingredients are evenly dispersed. Pour in the hot water and honey. Mix and form into a ball with your hands. (Dough should not be too sticky but hold well together in a ball. When flattened into a disk, it should not crack too much. Add small additions of water or quinoa flakes, if necessary.)

Place the disk (or divide into two disks, if easier) between the two pieces of parchment, lightly dust both sides and roll 1⁄16 inch (1.5 mm) thick. For a thicker cracker, ⅛ inch (3 mm) is acceptable but will need to be baked longer. Check frequently for sticking and dust with flour where required. Peel away the top parchment and place dough on the baking sheet. Sprinkle with sea salt. Bake in the preheated oven for 10 minutes. Remove the baking sheet from the oven. Place the second piece of parchment on top of the cracker dough again and flip. Remove the top parchment and cut into 1-inch (2.5 cm) wide strips with a pizza wheel or knife. Place the bottom parchment and crackers on the baking sheet (it is fine if crackers separate) and bake for another 7 to 10 minutes, depending on the thickness of your cracker. Watch closely in the last 5 minutes to prevent burning. Remove any crackers on the edges of the parchment that are getting too browned. Crackers should be fairly dry and slightly golden when done. Remove from the oven to cool and dry completely (to get crispy), especially if they are slightly chewy. Store crackers in a sealable container.

PER SERVING (4 crackers): Energy 130 calories; Protein 3 g; Carbohydrates 18 g; Dietary Fiber 2 g; Fat 6g; Sugar 3 g; Cholesterol 0 mg; Sodium 240 mg.

BASIL & WHITE BEAN AMARANTH DIP

MAKES 2 CUPS (500 ML), SERVES 8

Full of fiber and flavor, puréed beans are mixed with amaranth, toasted pine nuts, garlic, lemon and fresh basil leaves. No need to feel guilty indulging in this low-calorie and tasty dip. Enjoy with corn tortillas, carrot sticks or light-tasting crackers.

½ cup (125 mL) water
¼ cup (60 mL) amaranth seeds
1½ cups (375 mL) cooked white kidney beans
2 Tbsp (30 mL) fresh basil
½ cup (125 mL) toasted pine nuts
1 tsp (5 mL) minced garlic
¼ cup (60 mL) freshly squeezed lemon juice
2 Tbsp (30 mL) extra virgin olive oil
Pinch of salt
Pinch of white pepper

In a small saucepan, bring the water and amaranth to a boil. Reduce to a simmer and cook, covered, for 30 minutes. Remove from the heat and cool. Place amaranth, beans, basil, pine nuts, garlic, lemon juice, oil, salt and white pepper in food processor and pulse until smooth. Reseason if desired. Serve with vegetables or light-tasting crackers.

PER SERVING: Energy 140 calories; Protein 4 g; Carbohydrates 12 g; Dietary Fiber 3 g; Fat 9 g; Sugar 1 g; Cholesterol 0 mg; Sodium 60 mg.

- Alternatively, substitute ¾ cup (175 mL) cooked quinoa or sorghum for the amaranth.
- You can substitute navy or great northern beans for the white kidney beans.

RED PEPPER CHIPOTLE SUPERBLEND HUMMUS

MAKES 2 CUPS (500 ML), SERVES 8

Smoked chipotle flavor with roasted sweet red pepper makes this superblend hummus a delicious and unique appetizer! This tasty hummus made of ancient grains is a perfect accompaniment for crackers, veggies, sandwiches or tortillas.

⅔ cup (150 mL) water
3 Tbsp (45 mL) quinoa seeds
2 Tbsp (30 mL) millet seeds
1 Tbsp (15 mL) amaranth seeds
1 cup (250 mL) cooked chickpeas
¼ cup (60 mL) freshly squeezed lemon juice
2 Tbsp (30 mL) tahini
2 tsp (10 mL) minced garlic
2 Tbsp (30 mL) extra virgin olive oil
½ tsp (2 mL) ground chipotle pepper
½ cup (125 mL) roasted red peppers

Bring the water and grains to a boil in a small saucepan. Reduce to a simmer and cook, covered, for 20 minutes or until tender. Remove from the stove and cool completely. Place the grains, chickpeas, lemon juice, tahini, garlic, oil, ground chipotle and red peppers in a food processor and pulse until smooth. Reseason if desired.

PER SERVING: Energy 120 calories; Protein 3 g; Carbohydrates 12 g; Dietary Fiber 2 g; Fat 6 g; Sugar 1 g; Cholesterol 0 mg; Sodium 75 mg.

- You can use 1 cup (250 mL) cooked combination of amaranth, sorghum or kañiwa instead of the quinoa, millet and amaranth.

MANGO, CUCUMBER & RED PEPPER QUINOA SALAD

SERVES 4

Enjoyed any time of the year, this salad has a crisp, fresh cucumber flavor with sweet mangos and bold red pepper that is always in season. Wrap in rice paper for a simple and snazzy handheld lunch or appetizer.

1½ cups (375 mL) water
¾ cup (175 mL) quinoa seeds
¾ cup (175 mL) thinly sliced
    or diced mango
¾ cup (175 mL) thinly sliced
    or diced cucumber
½ cup (125 mL) red bell pepper,
    thinly sliced into 1-inch (2.5 cm)
    lengths
⅓ cup (75 mL) finely chopped
    toasted salted peanuts
¼ cup (60 mL) minced red onion
¼ cup (60 mL) apple cider vinegar
¼ cup (60 mL) extra virgin
    olive oil
2 tsp (10 mL) liquid honey
1 Tbsp (15 mL) chopped fresh
    cilantro (optional)
Pinch of salt (optional)

In a medium saucepan, bring the water and quinoa to a boil. Reduce to a simmer, cover and cook for 13 minutes. Remove cover and cool completely.

Place cooked quinoa in a medium bowl with mango, cucumber, red pepper, peanuts and red onion. In a small bowl, whisk together the vinegar, oil, honey, cilantro (if using) and salt (if using). Toss dressing with the quinoa mixture. Serve.

PER SERVING: Energy 360 calories; Protein 9 g; Carbohydrates 34 g; Dietary Fiber 5 g; Fat 22 g; Sugar 9 g; Cholesterol 0 mg; Sodium 45 mg.

> For a totally different salad, why not try an ancient grain blend of equal amounts of quinoa, millet, and buckwheat or 2 cups (500 mL) of cooked and drained sorghum?

CUCUMBER, CASHEW, QUINOA & BUCKWHEAT SALAD WITH MINT

SERVES 4

Fresh salad makes you feel good. Enjoy this buckwheat salad mixed with crisp cucumber, carrot, mint and sweet honey with tangy lime. Another great lunch option or a strikingly handsome appetizer if you wrap it in rice paper or tuck it in a small pita half.

In a medium saucepan, combine the water, quinoa and buckwheat and bring to a boil. Reduce to a simmer, cover and cook for 15 minutes. Remove from the heat. Fluff with a fork to cool completely.

Place the cooled grains in a medium bowl and add the cucumber, carrot, green onion and mint. In a small bowl, whisk together the oil, vinegar, lime juice, honey and salt (if using). Toss the dressing mixture with the salad, distributing evenly. Place in a serving bowl and sprinkle with cashews just before serving.

PER SERVING: Energy 300 calories; Protein 6 g; Carbohydrates 35 g; Dietary Fiber 5 g; Fat 16 g; Sugar 4 g; Cholesterol 0 mg; Sodium 20 mg.

Try this salad with 3 cups (750 mL) cooked and rinsed sorghum in place of the quinoa and buckwheat.

2 cups (500 mL) water

½ cup (125 mL) quinoa seeds

½ cup (125 mL) buckwheat groats

1½ cups (375 mL) diced seeded English cucumber

½ cup (125 mL) finely diced carrot

⅓ cup (75 mL) sliced green onion

¼ cup (60 mL) chopped fresh mint

¼ cup (60 mL) unrefined organic canola oil

2 Tbsp (30 mL) rice vinegar or white wine vinegar

2 Tbsp (30 mL) freshly squeezed lime juice

1 tsp (5 mL) liquid honey

¼ tsp (60 mL) salt (optional)

¼ cup (60 mL) toasted salted or unsalted cashews

FRESH CORN & MILLET BEAN SALAD WITH THYME VINAIGRETTE

SERVES 6

Raw corn adds a crisp texture and sweet flavor to this salad along with fresh green beans, cherry tomatoes and a savory thyme mustard vinaigrette.

2 cups (500 mL) water

1 cup (250 mL) millet seeds

1 cup (250 mL) fresh Italian flat or French green beans, quartered

1½ cups (375 mL) cooked red kidney beans, or 1 can (14 oz/398 mL), drained and rinsed

1½ cups (375 mL) cooked Romano beans, or 1 can (14 oz/398 mL), drained and rinsed

1¼ cups (300 mL) fresh sweet corn kernels (about 2 small cobs), cut off the cob and silks removed

1 cup (250 mL) diced green bell pepper

1 cup (250 mL) sweet cherry tomatoes, halved

⅓ cup (75 mL) finely diced Spanish onion

THYME VINAIGRETTE

⅓ cup (75 mL) extra virgin olive oil

⅓ cup (75 mL) freshly squeezed lemon juice

4 tsp (20 mL) mild Dijon mustard

2 tsp (10 mL) minced garlic

4 tsp (20 mL) chopped fresh thyme

1 tsp (5 mL) pure maple syrup or liquid honey

¼ tsp (1 mL) salt (optional)

¼ tsp (1 mL) freshly ground black pepper

In a medium saucepan, bring the water and millet to a boil. Reduce to a simmer, cover and cook for 15 minutes. Millet should be tender and slightly firm but not mushy. Remove from the heat and drain any remaining water. Fluff with a fork and cool completely.

Steam the green beans until tender but still crisp. Cool completely.

In a medium bowl, combine cooled millet, green beans, red kidney beans, Romano beans, corn, green pepper, tomatoes and Spanish onion.

For the dressing, in a small bowl, whisk together the oil, lemon juice, mustard, garlic, thyme, maple syrup, salt (if using) and pepper. Toss with salad. Serve.

PER SERVING: Energy 400 calories; Protein 13 g; Carbohydrates 57 g; Dietary Fiber 15 g; Fat 15 g; Sugar 6 g; Cholesterol 0 mg; Sodium 340 mg.

If you don't have millet or want a different version of this salad, cook an equal amount of quinoa, amaranth or kañiwa.

MANDARIN EDAMAME RED QUINOA SALAD

SERVES 4

Edamame, red pepper and quinoa, combined with tender mandarin pieces and a tangy dressing, make for a colorful and welcome addition to any barbecue, lunch or dinner plate. The quinoa and edamame help keep you feeling full longer. Red quinoa makes for a more dramatic presentation, but you can use black quinoa or alternative grains too.

Bring the water and quinoa to a boil. Reduce to a simmer, cover and cook for 13 to 15 minutes (the quinoa should be tender with a slight chewiness). Remove from the heat and cool completely.

Add the cooled quinoa to a medium bowl with the edamame, red pepper and green onion. In a small bowl, whisk together the oil, vinegar, tamari, ginger, garlic, maple syrup and 1 tsp (5 mL) reserved mandarin juice.

Toss with the quinoa mixture until evenly distributed. Gently toss in the mandarin segments. Sprinkle with sesame seeds and serve.

PER SERVING: Energy 370 calories; Protein 10 g; Carbohydrates 41 g; Dietary Fiber 6 g; Fat 19 g; Sugar 9 g; Cholesterol 0 mg; Sodium 80 mg.

> For variety, use 3 cups (750 mL) of cooked of millet, kañiwa or either superblend from page 3.

2 cups (500 mL) water

1 cup (250 mL) red quinoa seeds

1 cup (250 mL) thawed frozen shelled organic edamame

⅔ cup (150 mL) diced red bell pepper

⅓ cup (75 mL) thinly sliced green onion

¼ cup (60 mL) organic unrefined canola or walnut oil

2 Tbsp (30 mL) rice wine vinegar

2 tsp (10 mL) gluten-free tamari or soy sauce

1 tsp (10 mL) freshly grated ginger

½ tsp (2 mL) minced garlic

1 tsp (5 mL) pure maple syrup or liquid honey

1 can (10 oz/284 mL) mandarin orange segments, drained, juice reserved

1 Tbsp (15 mL) toasted sesame seeds

SPICY RED QUINOA SALAD

SERVES 4

Flexitarian, or simply trying to eat more lean meat alternatives? Delicious spiced Mexican taste and a meaty texture make this quinoa salad a well-seasoned alternative to the traditional meat version of a taco salad.

2 cups (500 mL) beef broth
    or vegetarian substitute
1 cup (250 mL) red or black
    quinoa seeds
1 tsp (5 mL) chili powder
½ tsp (2 mL) smoked or regular
    sweet paprika
½ tsp (2 mL) dried oregano
½ tsp (2 mL) minced garlic
¼ tsp (1 mL) ground cumin
¼ tsp (1 mL) freshly ground
    black pepper
¼ tsp (1 mL) salt (optional)
Pinch of cayenne or ground
    chipotle pepper
½ tsp (2 mL) unsalted butter
    (optional)
6 cups (1.5 L) baby spinach
1½ cups (375 mL) chopped fresh
    tomatoes
¾ cup (175 mL) shredded low-fat
    Cheddar cheese
¾ cup (175 mL) low-fat sour cream
½ cup (125 mL) sliced green onion

In a medium saucepan, bring the broth, quinoa, chili powder, paprika, oregano, garlic, cumin, pepper, salt (if using) and cayenne to a boil. Reduce to a simmer, cover and cook for 15 minutes. Remove from the heat. Stir in the butter, if using.

Divide the baby spinach between four plates and sprinkle ½ cup (125 mL) of hot seasoned quinoa over each. Top with tomatoes, Cheddar, sour cream and green onion. Serve immediately.

PER SERVING: Energy 310 calories; Protein 17 g; Carbohydrates 40 g; Dietary Fiber 7 g; Fat 10 g; Sugar 3 g; Cholesterol 20 mg; Sodium 280 mg.

SORGHUM PERSILLADE

SERVES 6

Inspired by French cuisine, persillade (parsley and garlic) has become a staple accompaniment for almost any meat or fish. Our sorghum version is an easy and versatile side dish that can be eaten cold or hot. Refrigerate for at least an hour or overnight for best flavor. Parsley is said to be good for detoxifying the body, aiding in proper digestion, preventing inflammation and freshening breath, and is even a good source of iron.

4 cups (1 L) water

1½ cups (375 mL) sorghum grains

1 cup (250 mL) minced fresh
    parsley

½ cup (125 mL) extra virgin
    olive oil

⅓ cup (75 mL) freshly squeezed
    lemon juice

1½ tsp (7 mL) lemon zest

1 tsp (5 mL) minced garlic

1 tsp (5 mL) liquid honey or pure
    maple syrup (optional)

¾ tsp (3 mL) salt (optional)

Freshly ground black pepper
    to taste

In a medium saucepan, bring the water and sorghum to a boil. Reduce to a simmer, cover and cook for 60 minutes or until sorghum is tender. Remove from the heat, drain and cool completely.

Place the cooled sorghum in a medium bowl and add the parsley, olive oil, lemon zest, lemon juice, garlic, honey (if using), salt (if using) and pepper. Refrigerate for an hour or more for best flavor.

PER SERVING: Energy 330 calories; Protein 6 g; Carbohydrates 38 g; Dietary Fiber 3 g; Fat 20 g; Sugar 0 g; Cholesterol 0 mg; Sodium 15 mg.

As an alternative, use quinoa instead, cooked in only 3 cups (750 mL) of water.

ROASTED CORN & RED PEPPER MILLET SALAD WITH SMOKED PAPRIKA DRESSING

SERVES 4

There is something wonderful about the smoked, sweet flavor of grilled vegetables. Toss them in a dressing of paprika, lime and Dijon with a touch of cilantro and millet and you have a spectacular salad.

Combine the water and millet in a medium saucepan and bring to a boil. Reduce to a simmer, cover and cook for 10 minutes. Remove from the heat and let sit, covered, for 5 minutes. Cool completely.

Preheat the barbecue to approximately 400°F (200°C). Place the corn cobs and whole red pepper on the grill. Barbecue until the corn has darkened about 10% and the red pepper has blackened 50% to 70%. Remove vegetables from the grill and place the red pepper in a sealed paper bag for about 15 minutes. Cut the kernels from the cob and remove the skin from the pepper. Dice the pepper and place in a medium bowl with the millet and corn.

Whisk together the oil, lime juice, cilantro, Dijon, maple syrup, paprika and salt. Pour over the vegetable mixture. Toss and serve.

PER SERVING: Energy 310 calories; Protein 5 g; Carbohydrates 28 g; Dietary Fiber 3 g; Fat 20 g; Sugar 5 g; Cholesterol 0 mg; Sodium 360 mg.

1 cup (250 mL) water

½ cup (125 mL) millet seeds

2 cobs of corn (small to medium, husks and silk removed, approx. 1 cup/250 mL kernels)

1 red bell pepper

⅓ cup (75 mL) extra virgin olive oil

¼ cup (60 mL) freshly squeezed lime juice

1 Tbsp (15 mL) chopped fresh cilantro

2 tsp (10 mL) Dijon mustard

2 tsp (10 mL) pure maple syrup or liquid honey

¼ tsp (1 mL) smoked or regular sweet paprika

½ tsp (2 mL) salt

Ancient grain options: Bring ¼ cup (60 mL) quinoa and ¼ cup (60 mL) buckwheat to a boil with 1 cup (250 mL) water. Cover and cook for 20 minutes. Cool completely and use instead of the millet in this salad.

WALNUT & BROCCOLI SUPERBLEND SALAD

SERVES 4

Crunchy and fresh, broccoli and walnuts are a delectable combination for a salad—and for your health! Broccoli will nourish and detox, while walnuts are full of healthy fiber, protein and good-for-you fats. And leftovers for lunch! This makes a great salad for the next day too.

Combine the water, buckwheat and quinoa in a small saucepan and bring to a boil. Reduce to a simmer, cover and cook for 15 minutes. Remove from the heat, fluff with a fork and cool completely.

Heat a sauté pan on medium heat and place the walnuts in the pan. Stir frequently until the walnuts are fragrant and toasted. Remove from the heat, cool slightly and coarsely chop. Set aside.

Place completely cooled grains, broccoli, walnuts, cranberries and red onion in a large bowl. Whisk together the honey, vinegar, oil, garlic and salt (if using). Toss with the vegetable mixture and serve.

PER SERVING: Energy 360 calories; Protein 8 g; Carbohydrates 47 g; Dietary Fiber 6 g; Fat 18 g; Sugar 21 g; Cholesterol 0 mg; Sodium 20 mg.

> Prefer cooked broccoli? Blanch the broccoli in boiling water for 2 minutes. Drain on a clean dish towel and cool completely before adding to the salad.

1 ⅓ cups (325 mL) water
⅓ cup (75 mL) buckwheat groats
⅓ cup (75 mL) quinoa seeds
½ cup (125 mL) walnuts
3 cups (750 mL) broccoli pieces
   (broccoli florets and peeled
   diced stalk)
⅓ cup (75 mL) dried sweetened
   cranberries
⅓ cup (75 mL) finely diced
   red onion
¼ cup (60 mL) liquid honey
   or pure maple syrup
¼ cup (60 mL) red wine vinegar
2 Tbsp (30 mL) olive or walnut oil
½ tsp (2 mL) minced garlic
Pinch of salt (optional)

ASPARAGUS & SWEET BABY PEA QUINOA PILAF WITH PARMESAN CHEESE

SERVES 4

Asparagus and sweet baby peas make a light and tasty pilaf, full of fresh green vegetables, that can be either a side dish or a complete meal. A dusting of grated Parmesan cheese adds a dash of buttery flavor.

1 lb (450 g) asparagus, ends trimmed

2 Tbsp (30 mL) unsalted butter

1 cup (250 mL) diced onion

1 tsp (5 mL) minced garlic

1 cup (250 mL) quinoa seeds (preferably white/golden)

4 cups (1 L) low-sodium chicken stock

¼ cup (60 mL) white wine

1 cup (250 mL) sweet baby peas

1 oz (28 g) freshly grated Parmesan cheese, plus additional for garnish

1 Tbsp (15 mL) chopped fresh thyme

¼ to ½ tsp (1 to 2 mL) salt

Freshly cracked black pepper (optional)

Blanch asparagus for 3 minutes in boiling water, then cool in cold water. Cut into thirds. Set aside.

Melt butter in large, wide-bottomed saucepan on medium-low heat. Add onion and cook for 5 minutes or until just starting to soften. Add the garlic and heat for 1 minute. Add the quinoa and stir. Let it heat and toast for 3 minutes. Stir in the chicken stock and wine. Bring to a boil, reduce to a simmer and cover. Simmer for 17 minutes or until quinoa is tender.

Stir in the peas, Parmesan cheese, thyme and salt. Add the asparagus and heat on low until hot. Garnish with additional Parmesan and cracked pepper if desired. Serve.

PER SERVING: Energy 350 calories; Protein 18 g; Carbohydrates 44 g; Dietary Fiber 8 g; Fat 12 g; Sugar 4 g; Cholesterol 20 mg; Sodium 330 mg.

TARRAGON & BROWN BUTTER SUPERBLEND VEGETABLE PILAF

SERVES 4

Brown butter has a rich, nutty taste and is easy to make. Toss it with fresh tarragon, white wine and cooked vegetables for a wonderful pilaf bursting with flavor.

In a small saucepan, melt the butter on medium heat, whisking constantly. Watch closely as brown flecks begin to appear. The butter will turn a caramel brown and have a nutty fragrance. This step should take 4 to 6 minutes (if the butter turns black, start over). Remove from the heat immediately and use a spatula to remove all the butter into a small bowl to prevent further heating. Set aside.

Heat a large saucepan or 12-inch (30 cm) sauté skillet with lid on medium low heat. Add the oil and onion. Cook for 7 minutes or until the onion starts to become tender. Stir in the buckwheat and quinoa and toast for 3 to 5 minutes, until the grains smell toasted. Sprinkle in the peas, carrots, broth, water and white wine. Simmer, covered, for 15 minutes. Remove from the heat; stir in the brown butter and tarragon. Reseason if desired and serve.

PER SERVING: Energy 240 calories; Protein 5 g; Carbohydrates 28 g; Dietary Fiber 5 g; Fat 11 g; Sugar 4 g; Cholesterol 15 mg; Sodium 60 mg.

2 Tbsp (30 mL) unsalted butter

1 Tbsp (15 mL) grapeseed oil

½ cup (125 mL) chopped onion

⅓ cup (75 mL) buckwheat groats

⅓ cup (75 mL) quinoa seeds

1 cup (250 mL sugar snap peas, cut diagonally into ½-inch (1 cm) pieces

1 cup (250 mL) diced carrot

1 cup (250 mL) vegetable or chicken broth

1 cup (250 mL) water

⅓ cup (75 mL) white wine

2 Tbsp (30 mL) roughly chopped fresh tarragon

KALE & CRANBERRY BUCKWHEAT PILAF WITH TOASTED PECANS & THYME

SERVES 4

Kale lovers will be thrilled with this one! Kale and ancient grains blend delightfully well with cranberries, toasted pecans and thyme with a hint of fresh garlic. This pilaf is outstanding with the tender Savory Swedish Meatballs & Gravy (page 153).

2 cups (500 mL) water

½ cup (125 mL) buckwheat groats

½ cup (125 mL) millet seeds

⅓ cup (75 mL) chopped pecans

1 Tbsp (15 mL) grapeseed or vegetable oil

¾ cup (175 mL) diced Spanish onion

2 cups (500 mL) thinly sliced kale, ribs removed

1½ tsp (7 mL) dried thyme

1 tsp (5 mL) minced garlic

¼ to ½ tsp (1 to 2 mL) salt (optional)

½ cup (125 mL) sweetened dried cranberries

2 Tbsp (30 mL) unrefined walnut oil or light vegetable oil

Combine the water, buckwheat and millet in a medium saucepan. Bring to a boil. Reduce to a simmer, cover and cook for 15 minutes. Remove from heat, fluff with a fork and set aside.

Heat a Dutch oven or large skillet on medium heat. Toast the pecans, stirring frequently, until fragrant and toasted. Remove from the pan and set aside in a small bowl.

Reheat the Dutch oven or large skillet on medium-low heat and add the oil. When hot, add the onions and stir frequently until they start to soften, about 5 minutes. Stir in the kale, thyme, garlic and salt (if using) and cook until kale is tender, about 5 minutes. Stir in the cooked ancient grains, dried cranberries, pecans and walnut oil until evenly combined. Heat until hot. Serve with Savory Swedish Meatballs & Gravy (page 153).

PER SERVING: Energy 400 calories; Protein 8 g; Carbohydrates 54 g; Dietary Fiber 9 g; Fat 19 g; Sugar 13 g; Cholesterol 0 mg; Sodium 20 mg.

> Instead of buckwheat or millet, use equal amounts of quinoa.

MEXICAN AMARANTH PILAF

SERVES 4

An amaranth pilaf with the spicy, warm flavors of cumin and cayenne as well as crisp green pepper, fresh cilantro and tomato make this dish full of bold flavor, nutrition and fun. Serve as a side dish to Southwestern dishes or with the Chorizo Green Pepper & Millet Frittata on page 148 or the Chipotle Mango Salsa on Black Bean Sprout Tostadas on page 150.

Add the oil to a preheated medium saucepan over medium-low heat. Stir in the onion and cook for 5 to 7 minutes, until they begin to soften. Stir in the garlic, cumin, salt (if using), black pepper and cayenne and heat for 30 seconds. Stir in the amaranth and pour the tomato juice and water over top. Bring to a boil. Reduce to a simmer, cover and cook for 20 minutes. Remove lid and stir in the green pepper. Continue to simmer, uncovered, for an additional 10 minutes, stirring frequently. Remove from the heat and let sit for about 5 to 7 minutes before serving (this helps with the consistency of the amaranth). Stir in the chopped cilantro before serving.

PER SERVING: Energy 350 calories; Protein 12 g; Carbohydrates 58 g; Dietary Fiber 7 g; Fat 9 g; Sugar 8 g; Cholesterol 0 mg; Sodium 20 mg.

1 Tbsp (15 mL) grapeseed or vegetable oil

1 cup (250 mL) chopped onion

1 tsp (5 mL) minced garlic

¾ tsp (3 mL) ground cumin

¼ tsp (1 mL) salt (optional)

¼ tsp (1 mL) freshly ground black pepper

Pinch of cayenne pepper

1½ cups (375 mL) amaranth seeds

2 cups (500 mL) unsalted tomato juice

2 cups (500 mL) water

1 or 2 green bell peppers, chopped

2 to 3 Tbsp (30 to 45 mL) chopped fresh cilantro

CHORIZO & MEXICAN AMARANTH-STUFFED PEPPERS

Make it a meal by preparing the pilaf with whole green peppers. Fry ½ lb (225 g) of the chorizo sausage recipe on page 148. Stir in the pilaf and set aside. Slice the top inch (2.5 cm) off the top of 4 green bell peppers and remove the seeds and membrane. Blanch the peppers for 3 minutes in boiling water and drain upside down. Preheat the oven to 350°F (180°C). Reheat the pilaf and sausage mixture on medium-low heat until warm. Stand the peppers upright in a 9-inch (2.5 L) square glass baking dish. Stuff the peppers with the pilaf mixture and bake, covered, for 10 to 15 minutes, until hot. Serve with warm cornbread if desired.

CHEDDAR GARLIC ANCIENT GRAIN BISCUITS

MAKES 16 BISCUITS, 3 INCHES (8 CM) WIDE

Served hot, these cheesy, buttery garlic biscuits are delectable alongside your favorite salad, soup or stew. They are even tasty gently reheated the next day. Potato starch helps keep them gluten-free and gives them a lighter flavour. Potato starch is easily purchased in the baking or health section of your grocery, bulk or health food store.

½ cup (125 mL) oat flour

⅓ cup (75 mL) sorghum flour

⅓ cup (75 mL) potato starch or brown rice flour

¾ tsp (3 mL) xanthan gum

2 tsp (10 mL) baking powder

¼ tsp (1 mL) baking soda

1½ tsp (7 mL) garlic salt

3 Tbsp (45 mL) unsalted butter

½ cup (125 mL) shredded reduced-fat aged Cheddar cheese

1 Tbsp (15 mL) minced fresh parsley or 1 tsp (5 mL) dried parsley

¾ cup (175 mL) buttermilk

Preheat the oven to 400°F (200°C) and place a piece of parchment on a large baking sheet; set aside. Place the oven rack in the center.

Combine the oat flour, sorghum flour, potato starch, xanthan gum, baking powder, baking soda and garlic salt in a large bowl. Whisk until evenly distributed. Using a pastry cutter, cut in the butter until the mixture is in pea-sized bits. Stir in the Cheddar and parsley. Pour in the buttermilk and, using a large spoon, fold the mixture until just combined. Spoon by slightly heaping tablespoons (15 mL) onto baking sheet, 2 inches (5 cm) apart. Flour clean hands and reshape the edges and flatten to ½-inch (1 cm) thick disks. Bake in the preheated oven for 8 to 10 minutes, until the edges are slightly golden. Cool slightly and serve.

PER SERVING (per biscuit): Energy 60 calories; Protein 2 g; Carbohydrates 8 g; Dietary Fiber 1 g; Fat 3 g; Sugar 1 g; Cholesterol 5 mg; Sodium 135 mg.

No oat flour on hand? Remember, it's fast and easy to make homemade oat flour. See page 2.

SOUPS & STEWS

Earthy, warm and comforting, nothing is better in soup than the nutrition of whole ancient grains. Thickening soups is easy with ancient grains, whether making a creamy purée or a chunky, hearty stew. It can also mean reducing the fat and calories of traditional creamy soups. If you prefer a soup that has more broth and is not as thick, use grains and seeds that have already been cooked. Adding previously cooked grains and seeds to a soup or stew will reduce the amount of broth absorbed.

Ancient grains not only provide a variety of textures in soups and stews, but also add flavor to please your taste buds. Amaranth enhances the flavor and creaminess of the Cheddar Cauliflower Amaranth Soup with Sherry & Thyme (page 112), ancient grain sprouts add a beautiful, unique and tasty texture to the Vietnamese Vegetable Noodle Soup with Quinoa Sprouts (page 120), and Spicy Peanut Amaranth Vegetable Soup with Cilantro (page 111) is our take on an original Bolivian soup called *sopa de mani*. These soups are especially comforting during the cold winter months whether they are easy last-minute meals or enjoyed simmered and slow cooked.

ASIAN CABBAGE & RED PEPPER SPROUT SOUP

SERVES 4

Asian flavors inspire this warmly spiced and slightly tangy low-fat soup with vegetables, sprouts, ginger, sesame and garlic. A lovely vegetarian crowd pleaser!

1 Tbsp (15 mL) grapeseed or vegetable oil

8 oz (225 g) mushrooms, quartered

¾ cup (175 mL) thinly sliced carrots, cut diagonally

1½ tsp (7 mL) finely grated ginger

1 tsp (5 mL) toasted sesame oil

½ tsp (2 mL) finely chopped or grated garlic

4 cups (1 L) vegetable or chicken stock

1 cup (250 mL) savoy or napa cabbage, thinly sliced

½ cup (125 mL) thinly sliced red bell pepper (approx. 1½ inches/4 cm long and 1/16 inch/1.5 mm wide)

1 cup (250 mL) quinoa sprouts

1 to 2 Tbsp (15 to 30 mL) rice wine vinegar

Pinch of cayenne pepper (optional)

Salt

¼ to ⅓ cup (60 to 75 mL) thinly sliced green onion, cut diagonally

Heat a 2-quart (2 L) saucepan on low heat. Stir in the grapeseed oil, mushrooms and carrots. Stir and cook until mushrooms start to soften. Stir in the ginger, sesame oil and garlic. Stir and heat for 1 minute. Pour in the stock and cabbage. Cook until carrots and cabbage are tender, approximately 5 minutes. Add the red pepper and sprouts. Stir in the vinegar, cayenne (if using) and salt to taste. Serve in bowls, garnished with green onion.

PER SERVING: Energy 150 calories; Protein 4 g; Carbohydrates 20 g; Dietary Fiber 4 g; Fat 6 g; Sugar 6 g; Cholesterol 0 mg; Sodium 190 mg.

Use teff or amaranth sprouts in place of quinoa sprouts.

SPICY PEANUT AMARANTH VEGETABLE SOUP WITH CILANTRO

SERVES 4

This recipe is a modern version of a hearty Bolivian soup called *sopa de mani*. Traditional versions of this non-dairy recipe are usually made with beef or chicken, but it is easily made into a vegetarian soup with whatever vegetables you have available. Our version is made with the unique twist of amaranth, peanut butter, vegetables, chicken and fresh cilantro. Add as little (or as much) cayenne pepper as you would like.

Heat a large saucepan on medium-low and add the oil. Stir in the onion and cook for about 7 minutes, until softened. Stir in the garlic, carrots, potatoes, amaranth, stock and water. Bring to a boil and reduce to a simmer; cook, covered, for 20 minutes or until the amaranth has cooked and vegetables are tender. Stir in the chicken and green pepper and cook for an additional 3 minutes. Stir in the peanut butter until incorporated into the broth (this may take a few minutes). Stir in the cilantro and season to taste with cayenne, salt and black pepper.

PER SERVING: Energy 390 calories; Protein 25 g; Carbohydrates 34 g; Dietary Fiber 5 g; Fat 17 g; Sugar 5 g; Cholesterol 30 mg; Sodium 210 mg.

2 tsp (10 mL) grapeseed or vegetable oil

½ cup (125 mL) chopped yellow onion

2 cloves garlic, minced

1 cup (250 mL) sliced carrots

¾ cup (175 mL) diced potato

½ cup (125 mL) amaranth seeds

4 cups (1 L) low-sodium chicken or vegetable stock

2 cups (500 mL) water

1 cup (250 mL) diced cooked chicken breast (or other chicken meat)

½ cup (125 mL) chopped green bell pepper

⅓ cup (75 mL) natural smooth peanut butter

1 Tbsp (15 mL) chopped fresh cilantro

Cayenne pepper, salt and freshly ground black pepper to taste

CHEDDAR CAULIFLOWER AMARANTH SOUP WITH SHERRY & THYME

SERVES 4

Enjoy this savory soup with a sprinkle of chives across the top and crusty bread or artisan crackers on the side. Cooked and puréed amaranth makes a luxurious and creamy soup and also provides additional nutrition.

1 Tbsp (15 mL) grapeseed oil

1 cup (250 mL) chopped onion

1½ tsp (7 mL) chopped garlic

4 cups (1 L) low-sodium chicken or vegetable stock

2 cups (500 mL) peeled diced Yukon gold or red potatoes

2 cups (500 mL) cauliflower, chopped into 1–inch (2.5 cm) pieces

⅓ cup (75 mL) amaranth seeds

¼ cup (60 mL) sherry

2 tsp (10 mL) chopped fresh thyme

1 cup (250 mL) 1% milk or milk substitute

1½ cups (375 mL) shredded reduced-fat aged Cheddar cheese

½ tsp (2 mL) salt (optional)

Freshly ground black pepper to taste

Sliced chives to garnish (optional)

Heat a large saucepan on medium-low heat. Add the oil and onion. Cover and cook for about 7 minutes or until the onion is opaque. Stir in the garlic and heat for an additional minute. Stir in the stock, potatoes, cauliflower, amaranth, sherry and thyme. Bring to a boil, then reduce to a simmer. Cover and cook for 20 minutes. Purée with an immersion blender or in small batches with a standard blender until smooth. Stir in the milk and cheese. Add salt (if using) and season with pepper as desired. Heat until cheese has melted. Serve topped with chives if you wish.

PER SERVING: Energy 320 calories; Protein 19 g; Carbohydrates 41 g; Dietary Fiber 4 g; Fat 9 g; Sugar 8 g; Cholesterol 10 mg; Sodium 390 mg.

- Reserve 1 cup (250 mL) of cooked potato, cauliflower and ancient grain mixture after cooking for 20 minutes and before puréeing. Add it again after the remainder of the soup has been puréed to make for a chunkier version.
- If you don't have amaranth on hand or want a change of flavor, an equal amount of quinoa seeds or 2 cups (500 mL) of precooked sorghum grains are great ancient grain alternatives.

ROASTED CHICKEN, KALE & BUCKWHEAT SOUP

SERVES 4

Give your take-out menus the night off. Weeknight meals should be delicious, simple and healthy. This chunky soup is all that with precooked chicken, kale, buckwheat and sweet potato.

Heat a large saucepan on medium-low heat. Add the oil, onion, celery and garlic. Cook, covered, for about 7 minutes or until the vegetables are starting to soften, adding a tablespoon or two (15 to 30 mL) of water to the pan if the mixture starts to dry out. Pour in the stock, water, sweet potato, buckwheat, kale, bay leaf and thyme. Bring to a simmer and cook, covered, for 17 minutes or until sweet potato and buckwheat are tender. Add the chicken and simmer until hot, 3 to 5 minutes. Add pepper and salt (if using) to taste. Serve.

PER SERVING: Energy 250 calories; Protein 16 g; Carbohydrates 35 g; Dietary Fiber 5 g; Fat 6 g; Sugar 5 g; Cholesterol 20 mg; Sodium 260 mg.

- Instead of cooked chicken, use precooked low-fat Italian sausage if desired.
- Swap out the buckwheat with an equal amount of kañiwa seeds, quinoa seeds or ¾ cup (175 mL) cooked sorghum grains.

1 Tbsp (15 mL) grapeseed or vegetable oil

1 cup (250 mL) chopped onion

¾ cup (3 mL) chopped celery

1 tsp (5 mL) minced garlic

4 cups (1 L) chicken stock

1 cup (250 mL) water

2 cups (500 mL) roughly diced sweet potato

⅓ cup (75 ml) buckwheat groats

2 cups (500 mL) thinly sliced kale, ribs removed

1 bay leaf

1 Tbsp (15 mL) fresh thyme or 1 tsp (5 mL) dried thyme

1 cup (250 mL) roughly diced roasted chicken

Freshly ground black pepper to taste

Salt to taste (optional)

SMOKED HAM & LEEK AMARANTH CHOWDER

SERVES 4

Feel like you've tried all the "light" cream soups out there? Smoked ham with a fragrant bay leaf fills the kitchen with a wonderful aroma. It is a nourishing combination that will pick up your spirit and fill you with wholesomeness.

1 Tbsp (15 mL) grapeseed or
   vegetable oil
1¾ cups (425 mL) sliced leeks
   (white parts only)
1¼ cups (300 mL) sliced celery
5 cups (1.25 L) water
2 cups (500 mL) low-sodium
   chicken or turkey stock
2½ cups (750 mL) diced ham
   or smoked turkey
2 cups (500 mL) diced potato
⅓ cup (75 mL) amaranth seeds
1 bay leaf
½ cup (125 mL) half-and-half
   (5%) cream
1 Tbsp (15 mL) chopped
   fresh parsley
½ tsp (2 mL) salt (optional)
¼ tsp (1 mL) freshly ground
   black pepper

Heat a large saucepan on medium-low heat. Add the oil, leeks and celery and cook for 7 minutes, until the celery is tender. Pour in the water and stock. Stir in the ham, potato, amaranth and bay leaf. Bring to a boil on medium-high heat and reduce to a simmer. Cover and cook for 25 minutes. Remove the bay leaf. Stir in the cream, parsley, salt (if using) and pepper. Serve.

PER SERVING: Energy 330 calories; Protein 20 g; Carbohydrates 39 g; Dietary Fiber 5 g; Fat 12 g; Sugar 3 g; Cholesterol 40 mg; Sodium 640 mg.

TURKEY & CHUNKY VEGETABLE SUPERBLEND SOUP WITH BASIL

....

SERVES 4

Change up your regular vegetable soup into a *super* soup! All the goodness of a turkey vegetable soup with the twist of ancient grains, tomato and basil.

Heat a large saucepan on medium-low heat and add the oil. Stir in the carrots, celery and onion to the pot. Cook, covered, until the onion and celery start to soften, about 7 minutes. Stir in the stock, water, turkey, 1 cup (250 mL) tomatoes, ancient grains, basil and parsley. Bring to a boil on medium heat, reduce to a simmer and cook for 17 minutes. Add the remaining cup (250 mL) diced tomato and cook for another 8 minutes. Season with salt and pepper as desired and serve.

PER SERVING: Energy 250 calories, Protein 27 g, Carbohydrates 25 g, Dietary Fiber 4 g; Fat 6 g; Sugar 6 g; Cholesterol 50 mg; Sodium 150 mg.

1 Tbsp (15 mL) grapeseed or vegetable oil

¾ cup (175 mL) chopped carrots

¾ cup (175 mL) chopped celery

¾ cup (175 mL) chopped onion

4 cups (1 L) low-sodium chicken or turkey stock

2 cups (500 mL) water

2 cups (500 mL) diced cooked turkey or chicken

2 cups (500 mL) diced tomatoes, divided

2 Tbsp (30 mL) millet seeds

2 Tbsp (30 mL) buckwheat groats

2 Tbsp (30 mL) amaranth seeds

1 tsp (5 mL) dried basil

1 tsp (5 mL) dried parsley

Salt and freshly ground black pepper to taste

VIETNAMESE VEGETABLE NOODLE SOUP WITH QUINOA SPROUTS

SERVES 4

Inspired by Vietnamese cuisine, this soup will use up the veggies in your fridge. Quick, yet spectacular looking, just throw together sprouts, precut vegetables and some rice noodles with flavorful hot broth and you've got a healthy and easy supper. We recommend carrots, mushrooms, red pepper and quinoa sprouts, but feel free to create your own tasty combinations.

BROTH

½ cup (125 mL) chopped onion

1 Tbsp (15 mL) grapeseed or vegetable oil

2 tsp (10 mL) minced garlic

1 slice (¾ inch/2 cm) fresh ginger

1 cinnamon stick

¼ tsp (1 mL) fennel seeds or 1 pod of whole star anise

3 whole cloves

Pinch of ground cardamom (optional)

8 cups (2 L) vegetable or chicken broth

2 tsp (10 mL) gluten-free tamari or regular soy sauce

SOUP

6½ oz (180 g) rice vermicelli

Boiling water

1 cup (250 mL) paper-thin sliced carrot

½ to ¾ cup (125 to 175 mL) quinoa sprouts

1 cup (250 mL) thinly sliced red bell pepper

¾ cup (150 mL) thinly sliced mushrooms
(button, cremini, porcini)

½ cup (125 mL) thinly sliced sugar snap
or snow peas

4 wedges lime

Hoisin and/or sriracha hot sauce (optional)

1 Tbsp (15 mL) coarsely chopped cilantro, basil
and/or mint

To make the broth, in a large saucepan, cook onion in oil on medium-low heat until just starting to soften, approximately 5 minutes. Stir in the garlic, ginger, cinnamon stick, fennel seeds, cloves and cardamom (if using) and heat for 2 minutes. Pour in vegetable broth and tamari, cover and simmer for 20 minutes. Drain broth into a container, discard solids, and pour broth back into saucepan.

To make the soup, place the rice noodles in a bowl large enough to fit comfortably and pour in boiling water to cover. Let them sit for 4 minutes. Drain the water and cool noodles under cold running water. Drain again and divide between four 3½-cup (875 mL) serving bowls. Divide the carrots, sprouts, red pepper, mushrooms and peas among the bowls as desired.

Reheat broth if it has cooled too much. Divide boiling broth among bowls, about 2 cups (500 mL) each. Squeeze a lime wedge into each and season with hoisin and/or sriracha hot sauce if desired. Garnish with desired herbs. Eat immediately.

PER SERVING: Energy 270 calories; Protein 5 g; Carbohydrates 49 g; Dietary Fiber 4 g; Fat 4 g; Sugar 7 g; Cholesterol 0 mg; Sodium 410 mg.

> Create your own soup combinations with different broths and thinly sliced vegetables.

SAHARA STEW OVER SUPERBLEND GRAINS

SERVES 6

Spices of Morocco combine in this delightful gravy full of tender beef, sweet potato and chickpeas topped with a pinch of lemon zest and fresh parsley. Serve it over ancient grains and you have a fine dining dinner on a shoestring budget.

Combine the water and quinoa, millet, buckwheat and amaranth in a medium saucepan and bring to a boil. Reduce to a simmer, cover and cook for 20 minutes. Remove from the heat and fluff with a fork. Set aside and keep warm.

Heat a large, deep pan over high heat. Add the oil and place the steak into the pan, leaving 1½ inches (4 cm) between each piece. Season with pepper and caramelize two sides of each piece (approx. 2 minutes per side), in two batches if necessary. Set meat aside in a shallow bowl covered with foil.

Reduce the heat to medium-low, stir in the onion and celery and cook, covered, for about 7 minutes or until they start to soften, adding water if pan looks dry. Stir in and heat the garlic, turmeric, cinnamon and salt (if using) for about 1 minute. Stir in the tomato paste. Add the broth, sweet potato and bay leaf. Bring to a boil, reduce to a simmer, cover and cook for 10 minutes. Remove the lid and continue to simmer for another 10 minutes. Add the chickpeas and sirloin and simmer an additional 8 minutes. Serve stew over ancient grains with parsley and lemon zest lightly sprinkled on top.

PER SERVING: Energy 480 calories; Protein 38 g; Carbohydrates 42 g; Dietary Fiber 7 g; Fat 17 g; Sugar 6 g; Cholesterol 85 mg; Sodium 250 mg.

2 cups (500 mL) water
½ cup (125 mL) quinoa seeds
¼ cup (60 mL) millet seeds
3 Tbsp (45 mL) buckwheat groats or kañiwa seeds
1 Tbsp (15 mL) amaranth seeds or teff grains
2 Tbsp (30 mL) grapeseed or vegetable oil
1¼ lb (565 g) sirloin steak, trimmed and cut into 1-inch (2.5 cm) chunks
¼ tsp (1 mL) freshly ground black pepper
1 cup (250 mL) chopped onion
1 cup (250 mL) chopped celery
2 tsp (10 mL) minced garlic
1 tsp (5 mL) turmeric
½ tsp (2 mL) cinnamon
½ tsp salt (optional)
⅓ cup (75 mL) unsalted tomato paste
4 cups (1 L) low-sodium beef broth
2 cups (500 mL) sweet potato, cut into 1-inch (2.5 cm) chunks
1 bay leaf
1 cup (250 mL) cooked chickpeas
1 Tbsp (15 mL) fresh chopped parsley
1 Tbsp (15 mL) freshly grated lemon zest

COCONUT CURRY LENTIL & SPINACH SORGHUM STEW

SERVES 6

Something a little different for those chilly evenings after a hard day at work—creamy coconut with a hint of curry, spinach, lentils, tomatoes and of course sorghum.

1 Tbsp (15 mL) grapeseed or
    vegetable oil
1 cup (250 mL) chopped onion
1½ tsp (7 mL) curry powder
½ tsp (2 mL) ground cumin
½ tsp (2 mL) ground coriander
3 Tbsp (45 mL) tomato paste
1 lb (450 g) dried yellow lentils
    or yellow split peas, rinsed
4 cups (1 L) vegetable or chicken
    stock
2 cups (500 mL) water
1 cup (250 mL) light coconut milk
½ cup (125 mL) chopped ripe
    tomatoes
½ cup (125 mL) sorghum grains
1 cup (250 mL) chopped
    baby spinach
Salt and freshly ground black
    pepper to taste

Heat a large saucepan on medium-low heat and add the oil. Cook the onion until starting to soften, about 5 to 7 minutes. Stir in the curry powder, cumin, coriander and tomato paste. Heat for an additional minute. Stir in the lentils, stock, water, coconut milk, tomatoes and sorghum. Simmer, covered, for 45 minutes or until the lentils are tender. Stir in the spinach and heat until wilted. Reseason with salt and pepper if desired and serve.

PER SERVING: Energy 390 calories; Protein 20 g; Carbohydrates 64 g; Dietary Fiber 15 g; Fat 7 g; Sugar 6 g; Cholesterol 0 mg; Sodium 125 mg.

> You can substitute an equal amount of quinoa, kañiwa or amaranth for the sorghum after simmering lentil mixture for 20 minutes.

SAVORY SAUSAGE & LENTIL KAÑIWA STEW

SERVES 6

Made with protein-rich kañiwa and chunky sausage, vegetables and lentils, this is a filling dish that is well-rounded and mouthwatering. Only 30 minutes to prepare and an hour to cook—and worth every minute! Enjoy it on a cool fall evening or the coldest of winter days. Easily freeze unused portions for up to 1 month to enjoy at a moment's notice.

Heat a Dutch oven or large saucepan (4 quarts/4 L) on medium-low heat. Add 1 Tbsp (15 mL) of the oil and the sausage. Cook until brown and no longer pink inside. Cut into half-moon slices, then return to the saucepan. Add remaining tablespoon (15 mL) of oil, onion, celery and carrots. Cook for 7 minutes or until the celery and onion start to soften. Pour in the broth and water, then stir in the lentils. Bring to a simmer and cook, covered, for 30 minutes. Stir in the kañiwa, zucchini and 1 cup (250 mL) diced tomatoes. Cook, covered, for another 30 minutes. Stir in the remaining tomatoes, wine, parsley and salt (if using) and pepper. Simmer until heated through, 5 to 7 minutes. Serve.

PER SERVING: Energy 490 calories; Protein 36 g; Carbohydrates 57 g; Dietary Fiber 13 g; Fat 15 g; Sugar 9 g; Cholesterol 25 mg; Sodium 530 mg.

> Use ½ cup (125 mL) quinoa seeds, amaranth seeds or teff grains in place of the kañiwa.

2 Tbsp (30 mL) grapeseed or vegetable oil, divided

1 lb (450 g) reduced-fat mild Italian sausage

¾ cup (175 mL) chopped onion

¾ cup (175 mL) chopped celery

¾ cup (175 mL) chopped carrots

4 cups (1 L) low-sodium beef broth

4 cups (1 L) water

1 cup (250 mL) green lentils, cleaned and rinsed

½ cup (125 mL) red lentils, cleaned and rinsed

½ cup (125 mL) kañiwa seeds

2 cups (500 mL) diced zucchini

1 can (28 oz/796 mL) diced tomatoes with juice, divided

¾ cup (175 mL) red wine

1 Tbsp (15 mL) chopped fresh parsley

½ tsp (2 mL) salt (optional)

¼ tsp (1 mL) freshly ground black pepper

SPICY CREOLE QUINOA STEW

SERVES 4

Sure to warm you up in the winter, this hot and chunky stew is another simple recipe that is even easy enough to be made on a busy weeknight! Increase or decrease the spicy heat by adjusting the amount of cayenne pepper.

2 Tbsp (30 mL) grapeseed
   or vegetable oil, divided
2 boneless chicken breasts
   or 4 boneless thighs
¾ cup (175 mL) chopped onion
¾ cup (175 mL) chopped celery
¾ cup (175 mL) chopped green
   bell pepper
1½ tsp (7 mL) minced garlic
1 tsp (5 mL) ground cumin
½ tsp (2 mL) dried thyme
¼ tsp (1 mL) dried oregano
¼ tsp (1 mL) cayenne pepper
   (optional)
¼ tsp (1 mL) sweet paprika
4 cups (1 L) low-sodium chicken
   broth
1 can (14 oz/398 mL) diced
   tomatoes with juice
⅓ to ½ cup (75 to 125 mL)
   quinoa seeds
1 bay leaf
1 lb (450 g) cooked shrimp

Heat a large saucepan over medium heat. Add 1 Tbsp (15 mL) of the oil and cook the chicken until no longer pink. Place chicken in a bowl and set aside, covered with foil.

Reheat saucepan over medium-low heat. Add the remaining tablespoon (15 mL) of oil and stir in the onion and celery. Cook, covered, for 5 to 7 minutes, until celery and onions are starting to become tender, adding a tablespoon or two (15 to 30 mL) of water if the pan becomes dry. Stir in the green pepper, garlic, cumin, thyme, oregano, cayenne (if using) and paprika; heat with the vegetables for 30 seconds. Stir in the chicken broth, tomatoes, quinoa and bay leaf. Simmer, covered, for 15 minutes or until quinoa is tender. Cut the chicken into large dice. Add the chicken and shrimp, simmering until the shrimp and chicken are hot, 2 to 3 minutes.

PER SERVING: Energy 380 calories; Protein 44 g; Carbohydrates 23 g; Dietary Fiber 3 g; Fat 12 g; Sugar 6 g; Cholesterol 280 mg; Sodium 510 mg.

MEALS

Dinner has never been better! Reminiscent of old favorites, the addition of ancient grains to traditional meals can not only improve the flavor and texture but add a wholesome nutritional profile that cannot be beat. Another advantage of ancient grains is that they are easy to prepare in advance and cook quickly after a hard day's work. Who would have thought ancient could be so easy? Try Alfredo Vegetable Sorghum Casserole (page 144) or Kañiwa-Stuffed Chicken Breasts (page 133) if you want to prepare a dish in advance. Ideal for dinner guests and family gatherings, Cheddar Sweet Potato Pie with Red Quinoa & Mushrooms (page 147) or Grilled Barbecue Portobellos with Kañiwa, Spinach & Blue Cheese (page 141) are sure to satisfy and make delectable leftovers. Thin-Crust Vegetable Pizza with Fresh Basil (page 134) makes a perfect small dinner—or even just dinner for one, with leftovers for your lunch the next day.

CHIA & OAT TUNA MELT MUFFINS

MAKES 12 MUFFINS

This savory tuna muffin has tender celery and onion topped with melted Cheddar cheese. With a generous dose of omega-3s, these muffins make a nutritious and light snack, hot or cold, for an easy supper or a fabulous addition to your lunch box!

1 Tbsp (15 mL) chia seeds, ground or whole

⅓ cup (75 mL) boiling water

1 Tbsp (15 mL) grapeseed or vegetable oil

1 Tbsp (15 mL) water

1 cup (250 mL) finely diced onion

1 cup (250 mL) finely diced celery

¾ cup (175 mL) oat or sorghum flour

1 tsp (5 mL) cornstarch

1 tsp (5 mL) dry mustard

¼ tsp (1 mL) freshly ground black pepper

1 cup (250 mL) shredded reduced-fat aged Cheddar cheese, divided

2 cans (6 oz/170 g each) low-sodium flaked water-packed tuna, drained

1 large egg, beaten

1 large egg white, beaten

3 Tbsp (45 mL) chopped fresh parsley or 1 Tbsp (15 mL) dried parsley

Combine the chia and boiling water in a small bowl. Gently stir with a fork to ensure the seeds are evenly distributed. Set aside to thicken.

Heat a sauté pan on medium-low heat. Add the oil and water. Cook the onion and celery, covered, until tender, about 7 minutes. Remove from the heat and let cool.

Preheat the oven to 375°F (190°C) with the oven rack in the center position. Line a standard muffin tin with paper liners, or lightly grease or spray them with cooking oil. Whisk together the oat flour, cornstarch, mustard and pepper in a medium bowl. Stir in ½ cup (125 mL) of the cheese. Set aside.

In a medium bowl, mix together the cooked onion and celery, chia mixture, tuna, egg, egg white and parsley. Add the wet mixture to the dry and stir until evenly mixed. Divide the mixture evenly between the muffin liners and sprinkle the remaining ½ cup (125 mL) cheese over the top of each muffin. Bake in the preheated oven for 20 minutes or until golden brown on the edges and center is piping hot.

PER SERVING (1 muffin): Energy 100 calories; Protein 11 g; Carbohydrates 5 g; Dietary Fiber 1 g; Fat 4 g; Sugar 1 g; Cholesterol 30 mg; Sodium 90 mg.

- Don't have chia on hand? Instead of the chia and boiling water, use ½ cup (125 mL) sour cream.
- If using dried parsley, for best results, add it when you cook the celery and onion.

KAÑIWA-STUFFED CHICKEN BREASTS

SERVES 4

The delicate crunch of kañiwa, mixed with fresh feta and herbs de Provence, is wrapped up in a deliciously moist, flavor-packed chicken breast. Terrific served along with roasted or mashed sweet potato.

Lightly grease and line a 13- × 9-inch (3.5 L) baking pan with parchment. Preheat the oven to 400°F (200°C).

In a small saucepan, bring the water and kañiwa to a boil. Reduce to a simmer, cover and cook for 10 minutes. Turn the heat off and leave the covered saucepan on the burner for an additional 6 minutes. Remove the lid and fluff with a fork.

In a small bowl, mix the kañiwa, feta cheese, pepper and herbs de Provence. Stir in the egg and mix well.

Wash and gently dry chicken breasts and place between two pieces of wax paper or parchment. Roll with a rolling pin until flattened (or use a meat pounder, gently). Spoon the kañiwa mixture onto the center of each chicken breast, roll up and secure with one or two toothpicks. Place the rolled chicken breasts in the prepared baking pan. In a separate bowl, combine the grapeseed oil, lemon juice and salt. Drizzle mixture over each piece of chicken.

Bake on the center rack of the preheated oven for 20 minutes. Remove from the oven and let the chicken stand for 3 to 4 minutes. Remove toothpicks before serving.

PER SERVING: Energy 340 calories; Protein 33 g; Carbohydrates 10 g; Dietary Fiber 1 g; Fat 18 g; Sugar 1 g; Cholesterol 145 mg; Sodium 620 mg.

½ cup (125 mL) water

¼ cup (60 mL) kañiwa seeds

¾ cup (175 mL) crumbled
    feta cheese

¼ tsp (1 mL) freshly ground
    black pepper

1½ tsp (7 mL) dried herbs
    de Provence

1 large egg

4 boneless skinless chicken
    breasts

2 Tbsp (30 mL) grapeseed oil

1 Tbsp (15 mL) freshly squeezed
    lemon juice

¼ tsp (1 mL) salt

Substitute cooked quinoa, millet or teff for the kañiwa.

THIN-CRUST VEGETABLE PIZZA WITH FRESH BASIL

MAKES ONE 12-INCH (30 CM) PIZZA (6 TO 8 SLICES), SERVES 4

A thin and crispy pizza crust perfectly baked with spinach, red pepper, mozzarella, feta and fresh basil—or any of your personal favorite pizza toppings.

CRUST

⅓ cup (75 mL) sorghum flour

⅓ cup (75 mL) millet flour

½ cup (125 mL) light
    buckwheat flour

½ tsp (2 mL) xanthan gum

½ tsp (2 mL) salt

½ cup (125 mL) warm water

1 tsp (5 mL) liquid honey

1½ tsp (7 mL) quick-rise yeast

1 large egg white

1 to 2 Tbsp (15 to 30 mL) extra
    virgin olive oil

Light flour, such as white or brown
    rice flour, for rolling.

TOPPINGS

½ cup (125 mL) pizza sauce

1 Tbsp (15 mL) grapeseed oil

1½ cups (375 mL) thinly sliced
    mushrooms

1 sweet yellow bell pepper,
    thinly sliced

1 sweet red bell pepper,
    thinly sliced

½ cup (125 mL) thinly sliced onion

¼ cup (60 mL) thinly sliced
    baby spinach

⅓ cup (75 mL) sliced black olives

1 cup (250 mL) partly skimmed,
    low-sodium mozzarella cheese

½ cup (125 mL) reduced-fat
    feta cheese

2 Tbsp (30 mL) chopped
    fresh basil

Line a large baking sheet with parchment and set aside.

In a medium bowl, whisk the sorghum flour, millet flour, buckwheat flour, xanthan gum and salt until well combined.

In a small bowl, whisk together the warm water and honey. Sprinkle the yeast into the bowl, stir and let sit for 5 minutes. Whisk in the egg white and olive oil.

Pour over the flour mixture and stir until combined. Cover and let sit for 20 minutes. Preheat the oven to 400°F (200°C). Remove parchment from baking sheet and place on the counter or other firm surface. Remove dough from the bowl. Form into a disk and sprinkle with flour. Roll with a rolling pin into a 12-inch (30 cm) wide crust about ¼ inch (5 mm) thick (no need to flip crust). Grabbing opposite corners of the parchment, place it back on the baking sheet. Spread with pizza sauce and bake in the preheated oven for 5 minutes.

During this time, preheat a 10-inch (25 cm) sauté pan on medium heat and add the grapeseed oil. Stir in the mushrooms, yellow and red peppers and onion; cook, stirring, until onions are starting to soften, about 5 minutes. Remove from the heat and set aside. Remove crust from the oven and top with cooked vegetables. Sprinkle with spinach, olives, mozzarella and feta cheese.

Bake for 8 minutes or until the crust is golden on the bottom. Turn on broiler and place pizza under the broiler for a minute or two, until the cheese is melted and starting to brown. Remove from the oven and cut into slices. Sprinkle with chopped basil and serve immediately.

PER SERVING: Energy 430 calories; Protein 19 g; Carbohydrates 39 g; Dietary Fiber 7 g; Fat 24 g; Sugar 3 g; Cholesterol 20 mg; Sodium 490 mg.

THAI BEEF & VEGETABLE ANCIENT GRAIN WRAP

MAKES 6 WRAPS

Fresh Thai flavors of chile-fried beef, red peppers and mushrooms combined with creamy coconut ancient grains, mint, green onions and a ginger lime sauce. Make it as hot and spicy as you can handle.

In a medium saucepan, bring the coconut milk, millet and quinoa to a boil. Reduce to a simmer and cook, covered, for 15 minutes, until just tender. Remove from heat, fluff with a fork and set aside.

Heat a large sauté pan on medium heat and add the oil and minced chiles. Stir in the beef strips (in two batches, if necessary) and garlic and stir-fry until the beef is browned and no longer pink, 3 to 5 minutes. Remove meat from the pan and set aside in a bowl covered with foil. Add the mushrooms, red pepper and white onion (if using) to the saucepan and cook until softened, adding 1 or 2 Tbsp (15 to 30 mL) of water to the pan if it looks dry. Place in separate bowl covered with foil and set aside.

To make the sauce, in a small bowl, whisk together the soy sauce, lime juice, honey, ginger and sriracha sauce. Set aside.

Serve the wrap ingredients on the table so people can build their own. Place ⅓ cup (75 mL) of coconut-cooked grains on the wrap first, then a bit of the vegetable mixture, then some beef strips topped with green onions, mint leaves and sauce. Serve.

PER SERVING (1 wrap): Energy 380 calories; Protein 25 g; Carbohydrates 41 g; Dietary Fiber 5 g; Fat 13 g; Sugar 9 g; Cholesterol 40 mg; Sodium 540 mg.

- Don't want to use wraps? Place the coconut-cooked grains in a bowl and add toppings. Enjoy!
- No mint available? Replace with an equal amount of cilantro leaves.

2½ cups (625 mL) light coconut milk
½ cup (125 mL) millet seeds
½ cup (125 mL) quinoa seeds
1 Tbsp (15 mL) grapeseed or vegetable oil
2 to 3 red Thai chiles, minced, or ¼ tsp (1 mL) hot pepper flakes
1 lb (450 g) lean stir-fry beef strips
2 tsp (10 mL) minced garlic
7 oz (200 g) mushrooms, sliced
1 orange or red bell pepper, seeded and sliced
½ cup (125 mL) thinly sliced white onion (⅛-inch/3 mm slices) (optional)
6 brown rice (gluten-free) or whole wheat wraps
⅓ cup (75 mL) thinly sliced green onions
¼ cup (60 mL) whole fresh mint leaves

SAUCE

¼ cup (60 mL) light gluten-free tamari or regular soy sauce
3 Tbsp (45 mL) freshly squeezed lime juice
2 Tbsp + 1 tsp (35 mL) liquid honey
1 tsp (5 mL) freshly grated ginger
1 tsp (5 mL) sriracha hot sauce

GRILLED CHICKEN ON LIME AVOCADO QUINOA SALAD

SERVES 6

This zesty lime and creamy avocado salad is served on a bed of crisp lettuce. Top with crunchy tortillas and cheese, if desired. Just leave out the chicken for a vegetarian dish.

2 cups (500 mL) water

1 cup (250 mL) quinoa seeds

¼ cup (60 mL) unrefined organic canola oil

⅓ cup (75 ml) freshly squeezed lime juice (about 1½ limes)

1 Tbsp (15 mL) rice vinegar or apple cider vinegar

1 tsp (5 mL) liquid honey or pure maple syrup

¼ tsp (1 mL) ground cumin

¼ tsp (1 mL) salt

Pinch of cayenne pepper

2 Tbsp (30 mL) chopped fresh cilantro

1 avocado, diced

1 cup (250 mL) diced red bell pepper

⅓ cup (75 mL) minced red onion

3 boneless skinless chicken breasts

4 cups (1 L) romaine or iceberg lettuce, thinly sliced

¾ cup (175 mL) broken unsalted tortillas (gluten-free if required)

¼ cup (60 mL) shredded reduced-fat aged Cheddar cheese (optional)

Preheat the barbecue on high.

Combine the water and quinoa in a medium saucepan and bring to a boil. Reduce to a simmer, cover and cook for 13 minutes. Remove from the heat and let cool completely.

Whisk together the oil, lime juice, vinegar, honey, cumin, salt, cayenne and cilantro. Gently toss the avocado with the dressing and set aside.

Place the cooled quinoa, red pepper, red onion and avocado mixture in a medium bowl. Gently toss and set aside.

Grill chicken breasts until they reach 170°F (80°C) on an instant-read thermometer. Remove from grill and set aside for 7 to 10 minutes. Slice into ½-inch (1 cm) slices.

Place ¾ to 1 cup (175 to 250 mL) shredded lettuce on each plate and top with the avocado mixture. Top with slices of chicken breast, tortilla pieces and shredded Cheddar (if using). Serve immediately.

PER SERVING: Energy 410 calories; Protein 20 g; Carbohydrates 42 g; Dietary Fiber 7 g; Fat 19 g; Sugar 3 g; Cholesterol 40 mg; Sodium 180 mg.

Never under- or overcook your meat again! Use an an instant-read food thermometer to cook your meats safely and accurately.

GRILLED PORTOBELLOS WITH KAÑIWA, SPINACH & BLUE CHEESE

SERVES 4

Blue cheese has a distinct salty, sharp taste that pairs beautifully with the portobello, spinach and smoky barbecue flavor of this dish. Make it heavenly by adding toasted walnuts to the stuffing. Enjoy these stuffed mushrooms with a salad of mixed greens with shallot mustard dressing.

In a medium saucepan, bring the water and kañiwa to a boil. Reduce to a simmer and cook, covered, for 15 minutes. Remove from the heat and set aside.

Brush the tops of the mushroom caps with 1 Tbsp (15 mL) of the oil. Set on a tray or baking sheet.

Heat a sauté pan on medium heat. Toast the walnuts (if using) in the dry pan, stirring, until fragrant. Set aside walnuts to cool. Reduce heat to medium-low. Add last tablespoon (15 mL) of oil; stir in onion and chopped mushroom stems. Cook until onion is tender, about 7 minutes, adding a tablespoon (15 mL) of water if pan appears dry. Stir in spinach and heat until wilted.

Stir the cooked kañiwa, walnuts (if using) and blue cheese into the spinach mixture. Divide the mixture evenly between the mushrooms. Sprinkle the 2 Tbsp (30 mL) reserved blue cheese over the kañiwa filling.

Preheat the barbecue to approximately 450°F (230°C). Lightly grease the grill and barbecue mushrooms, cap side down, for 8 to 10 minutes, until cheese is melted and mushrooms are tender.

To make the salad, whisk together the oil, shallots, vinegar, Dijon and honey. Toss desired amount of dressing into greens and serve alongside a warm portobello.

PER SERVING: Energy 390 calories; Protein 11 g; Carbohydrates 27 g; Dietary Fiber 4 g; Fat 28 g; Sugar 5 g; Cholesterol 15 mg; Sodium 340 mg.

1 cup (250 mL) water

½ cup (125 mL) kañiwa seeds

4 portobello mushrooms, stems removed and chopped

2 Tbsp (30 mL) grapeseed or vegetable oil, divided

¼ cup (60 mL) coarsely chopped walnuts (optional)

⅔ cup (150 mL) onion, sliced ½ inch (1 cm) thick

3 cups (750 mL) baby spinach, chopped

½ to ¾ cup (125 to 175 mL) crumbled blue cheese, with 2 Tbsp (30 mL) reserved to sprinkle on top

SALAD

¼ cup (60 mL) unrefined walnut or extra virgin olive oil

1 Tbsp (15 mL) minced shallots

1½ Tbsp (22 mL) white wine vinegar

2 tsp (10 mL) mild Dijon mustard

1 tsp (5 mL) honey

4 to 6 cups (1 to 1.5 L) mixed greens

- If you would rather bake these beauties, bake on the center rack in a 450°F (230°C) oven for 10 minutes on a parchment-lined baking sheet.
- Instead of kañiwa, use 1½ cups (375 mL) of cooked multicolored quinoa or Superblend 1 or 2 (page 3).

BAKED SALMON AMARANTH CAKES WITH SMOKED PAPRIKA & LEMON CREAM

SERVES 4

Smoked paprika and lemon partners beautifully with salmon to create a delicious and nutritious meal you'll be glad you made. Serve with a side of steamed broccoli or green beans.

SALMON CAKES

1 cup (250 mL) water

⅓ cup (75 mL) amaranth seeds

1 can (7 oz/217 g) low-sodium wild Alaskan salmon

¾ cup (175 mL) grated potato

¼ cup (60 mL) minced red onion

2 large egg whites

2 Tbsp (30 mL) chopped fresh parsley or 2 tsp (10 mL) dried parsley

2 Tbsp (30 mL) mild Dijon mustard

1 Tbsp (15 mL) oat flour

¼ tsp (1 mL) salt (optional)

Pinch of freshly ground black pepper

SMOKED PAPRIKA & LEMON CREAM

½ cup (125 mL) 2% Greek yogurt

¼ cup (60 mL) light mayonnaise

½ tsp (2 mL) freshly grated lemon zest

1 Tbsp (15 mL) freshly squeezed lemon juice

½ tsp (2 mL) puréed garlic

¼ tsp (1 mL) smoked sweet paprika

Chives for garnish (optional)

For the salmon cakes, combine the water and amaranth in a small saucepan and bring to a boil. Reduce to a simmer, cover and cook for 20 minutes. Remove from the heat and rinse amaranth under cold water in a fine-mesh strainer.

Preheat the oven to 350°F (180°C) with oven rack in center position. Place a piece of parchment or a silicone mat on a large baking sheet and set aside.

Combine ¾ cup (175 mL) of the cooled amaranth with the salmon, potato, red onion, egg whites, parsley, Dijon, flour, salt (if using) and pepper in a medium bowl. Use clean hands to mix ingredients until evenly distributed. Scoop mixture with a ¼-cup (60 mL) measure and form into patties ¾ inch (2 cm) thick on the prepared baking sheet. Bake in the preheated oven for 18 minutes.

For the smoked paprika and lemon cream, mix the Greek yogurt, mayonnaise, lemon zest, lemon juice, garlic and paprika in a small bowl.

Remove the salmon cakes from the oven and serve each with 1 Tbsp (15 mL) of the cream, garnished with chives (if using).

PER SERVING: Energy 210 calories; Protein 17 g; Carbohydrates 23 g; Dietary Fiber 2 g; Fat 5 g; Sugar 4 g; Cholesterol 30 mg; Sodium 390 mg.

This recipe can also be made with ¾ cup (175 mL) cooked kañiwa, quinoa, teff or Superblend 1 or 2 (page 3).

ALFREDO VEGETABLE SORGHUM CASSEROLE

SERVES 6

This creamy Alfredo sauce is lighter than it tastes! Mix it with sorghum and vegetables for a completely delicious meal—and make this supper super simple by cooking the sorghum and chicken the night before.

2½ cups (625 mL) water

¾ cup (175 mL) sorghum grains

4 cups (1 L) frozen mixed vegetables (such as yellow and green beans with carrots)

2 cups (500 mL) 1% milk

2 Tbsp (30 mL) cornstarch

2 tsp (10 mL) dried parsley

2 tsp (10 mL) minced garlic

½ tsp (2 mL) salt (optional)

¼ tsp (1 mL) freshly ground black pepper

1½ cups (375 mL) freshly grated Parmesan cheese

2 Tbsp (30 mL) unsalted butter (optional)

2 cups (500 mL) large-diced cooked chicken

In a medium saucepan, bring the water and sorghum to a boil. Reduce to a simmer and cook, covered, for 60 minutes. Remove from the heat, drain and set aside.

Rinse the frozen vegetables briefly under hot running water to slightly thaw and remove any ice particles. Cut any large pieces into 2-inch (5 cm) lengths, if necessary.

In a medium saucepan, whisk together the milk, cornstarch, parsley, garlic, salt (if using) and pepper. Bring to a simmer on medium-low heat, stirring constantly. Cook for 1 minute after it reaches a simmer. It should thicken and easily coat the back of a spoon. Stir in the Parmesan and butter (if using) until melted. Reseason with salt and pepper if desired and set aside.

Preheat the oven to 350°F (180°C) with the oven rack in the center. Lightly grease a 9-inch (2.5 L) square casserole dish. Evenly spread the cooked sorghum on the bottom, then the mixed vegetables, then the chicken and top with the Alfredo sauce. Bake, uncovered, in the preheated oven for 30 minutes or until the vegetables are tender and the edges of the sauce are golden. Cool slightly before serving.

PER SERVING: Energy 340 calories; Protein 26 g; Carbohydrates 39 g; Dietary Fiber 7 g; Fat 9 g; Sugar 8 g; Cholesterol 45 mg; Sodium 580 mg.

Instead of sorghum, use 2¼ to 2½ cups (550 to 625 mL) of kañiwa or quinoa.

ROMANO & RAINBOW SWISS CHARD HERBED QUICHE WITH QUINOA CRUST

SERVES 4

Savory herbs, Romano cheese and sautéed rainbow Swiss chard make a delectable quiche with a healthy quinoa crust. Swiss chard is a good source of iron, potassium, magnesium and of course fiber. Fluffy quinoa makes for a lighter alternative than the crust used in a traditional quiche.

For the crust, in a small saucepan, bring the water and quinoa to a boil. Reduce to a simmer and cook, covered, for 20 minutes. Remove from the heat and cool. Preheat the oven to 375°F (190°C). Lightly grease a 9 inch (23 cm) round pie dish and set aside. Place 1⅔ cups (425 mL) of quinoa in a medium bowl and toss with cornstarch. Then coat with melted butter and stir in the egg white. Press evenly into prepared pie dish and bake for 5 minutes. Remove from the oven and set aside.

For the filling, heat a sauté pan on medium-low heat and add the oil. Cook the onion until softened, about 5 to 7 minutes. Stir in the chard and salt and cook until the chard is tender. Stir in the basil, thyme and garlic and cook for an additional 30 seconds. Remove from the heat and let cool.

Reheat the oven to 375°F (190°C), if necessary, and place the oven rack in the center position.

Whisk together the egg whites, whole eggs and milk. Set aside. Distribute the onion-chard mixture evenly in the crust. Sprinkle the cheese evenly over top. Pour the egg mixture into the crust. Bake for 40 to 45 minutes, until set (you can slide the dish from side to side and the filling is solid, not moving back and forth). Let it rest for 10 to 12 minutes, then run a knife between the edge of the quiche and pie plate. Cut into 4 wedges and serve.

PER SERVING: Energy 320 calories; Protein 18 g; Carbohydrates 24 g; Dietary Fiber 3 g; Fat 17 g; Sugar 6 g; Cholesterol 120 mg; Sodium 490 mg.

CRUST

1 cup (250 mL) water

½ cup (125 mL) quinoa seeds

1 Tbsp (15 mL) cornstarch

2 Tbsp (30 mL) melted butter

1 large egg white, beaten

FILLING

1 Tbsp (15 mL) grapeseed or vegetable oil

1 cup (250 mL) onion, thinly sliced (approx. ¼ inch/5 mm thick)

4 cups (1 L) rainbow Swiss chard, ribs removed, leaves chopped

Pinch of salt

2 Tbsp (30 mL) chopped fresh basil or 2 tsp (10 mL) dried basil

1½ Tbsp (22 mL) chopped fresh thyme or 1½ tsp (7 mL) dried thyme

½ tsp (2 mL) minced garlic

4 large egg whites

2 large eggs

1 cup (250 mL) 1% milk or half-and-half (5%) cream

⅓ to ½ cup (75 to 125 mL) freshly grated Romano or Parmesan cheese

CHEDDAR SWEET POTATO PIE WITH RED QUINOA & MUSHROOMS

SERVES 4

Aged Cheddar cheese melted on fluffy sweet potatoes, seasoned red quinoa and mushrooms makes for a superbly layered meal, especially when served over sweet baby peas, broccoli or green beans.

Place the sweet potatoes in a medium saucepan and cover with water. Cook until tender. When cool enough to handle, remove skins and mash until smooth. Cover and set aside.

In a small saucepan, bring the water and quinoa to a boil, then reduce to a simmer. Cover and cook for 15 minutes. Remove from the heat.

Preheat the oven to 350°F (180°C). Lightly grease a 9-inch (2.5 L) square casserole dish.

Heat a medium sauté pan over medium-low heat. Place oil and onions in the pan, cover and cook for 5 to 7 minutes, until softened (if the pan becomes noticeably dry, add 2 Tbsp/30 mL water). Stir in the mushrooms, thyme, marjoram, garlic, salt (if using) and pepper. Cook, covered, until mushrooms soften, about 5 minutes.

Stir in the cooked quinoa. Whisk the broth and cornstarch together and pour into the mushroom mixture. Stir constantly until the mixture thickens, about 1 minute after starting to boil.

Pour into the prepared casserole dish. Spoon the sweet potato over the top of the casserole, spreading evenly with the back of the spoon. Sprinkle the top with cheese. Bake, uncovered, for 25 to 30 minutes or until the pie is hot and cheese is bubbling. Serve over hot sweet baby peas, broccoli, edamame or green beans.

1½ lb (675 g) sweet potatoes, cut into 2-inch (5 cm) wide pieces
1 cup (250 mL) water
½ cup (125 mL) red quinoa seeds
1 Tbsp (15 mL) grapeseed or vegetable oil
¾ cup (175 mL) diced onion
7 oz (200 g) mushrooms, chopped
2 Tbsp (30 mL) chopped fresh thyme or 2 tsp (10 mL) dried thyme
½ tsp (2 mL) dried marjoram
½ tsp (2 mL) minced garlic
¼ tsp (1 mL) salt (optional)
¼ tsp (1 mL) freshly ground black pepper
2 cups (500 mL) beef broth or vegetarian beef-flavored broth (gluten-free, if required)
2 Tbsp + 1 tsp (35 mL) cornstarch
1 cup (250 mL) shredded reduced-fat aged white Cheddar cheese

PER SERVING: Energy 400 calories; Protein 17 g; Carbohydrates 51 g; Dietary Fiber 7 g; Fat 15 g; Sugar 11 g; Cholesterol 30 mg; Sodium 95 mg.

Can't find red quinoa? Try the same amount of multicolored or black quinoa instead.

CHORIZO & GREEN PEPPER MILLET FRITTATA

SERVES 4

Homemade low-fat chorizo turkey sausage and fluffy millet give this quick dinner superb flavor and texture without the excess calories. Serve with green salsa and warmed corn tortillas if desired.

1 cup (250 mL) water

½ cup (125 mL) millet seeds

1 Tbsp (15 mL) grapeseed or vegetable oil

½ lb (225 g) chorizo sausage meat (see recipe below)

1 cup (250 mL) chopped green bell pepper

6 large egg whites

3 large eggs

⅓ cup (75 mL) 1% milk

3 Tbsp (45 mL) sliced green onion

2 Tbsp (30 mL) chopped fresh cilantro

Salt and freshly ground pepper to taste (optional)

1 lb (450 g) lean ground turkey or chicken

2 tsp (10 mL) chili powder

1½ tsp (7 mL) sweet or smoked sweet paprika

¼ to ½ tsp (1 to 2 mL) cayenne pepper

1 tsp (5 mL) minced garlic

½ tsp (2 mL) salt (optional)

½ tsp (2 mL) freshly ground black pepper

½ tsp (2 mL) dried oregano

¼ tsp (1 mL) ground cumin

Pinch of ground cloves

Pinch of cinnamon

2 Tbsp (30 mL) apple cider vinegar or white vinegar

In a small saucepan, bring the water and millet to a boil. Reduce to a simmer, cover and cook for 15 minutes. Remove from the heat and drain any remaining water. Fluff with a fork and set aside to cool.

Heat a 10-inch (25 cm) ovenproof skillet on medium heat and add the oil. Cook the sausage until browned and no longer pink. Reduce the heat to medium-low, stir in the green pepper and cook for another 7 minutes, until the pepper is tender. Whisk the cooled millet with the egg whites, whole eggs and milk.

Preheat the broiler.

Pour egg mixture over the sausage and green pepper. Cook the mixture, gently stirring and lifting the eggs from the sides, until eggs begin to set. Place the skillet under the broiler for a few minutes to finish cooking the eggs. Sprinkle with green onion, cilantro and salt and pepper (if using). Cut into 4 servings and enjoy.

HOMEMADE LOW-FAT CHORIZO SAUSAGE

Make this sausage to freeze raw or cooked. Either way, it will be a flavorful addition to your regular healthy recipe ingredients. Form into patties to make a scrumptious breakfast.

In a large bowl, combine turkey, chili powder, paprika, cayenne, garlic, salt (if using), black pepper, oregano, cumin, cloves, cinnamon and vinegar. Form into sausages, chunks or patties; cook in a lightly oiled sauté pan over medium heat until browned and no longer pink. Use as desired.

PER SERVING: Energy 400 calories; Protein 37 g; Carbohydrates 24 g; Dietary Fiber 6 g; Fat 17 g; Sugar 3 g; Cholesterol 220 mg; Sodium 240 mg.

CHIPOTLE MANGO SALSA ON BLACK BEAN SPROUT TOSTADAS

SERVES 6

This smoky Chipotle Mango Salsa is fresh and full of flavor, nicely accented with creamy, mild Gouda cheese, delicate sprouts, crisp shredded iceberg lettuce and earthy black beans, all on a crisp tortilla.

2¼ cups (550 mL) quinoa sprouts (page 5)

CHIPOTLE MANGO SALSA

1 ripe mango
1½ cups (375 mL) diced plum (Roma) tomatoes
¼ cup (60 mL) finely diced red onion
1 to 2 Tbsp (15 to 30 mL) chopped fresh cilantro
2 Tbsp (30 mL) freshly squeezed lime juice
1½ tsp (7 mL) finely chopped chipotle peppers
    in adobo sauce
¼ tsp (1 mL) puréed garlic
Pinch of salt

BLACK BEAN TOSTADAS

1 can (19 oz/540 mL) black beans, rinsed
¼ cup (60 mL) finely minced red onion
2 to 3 Tbsp (30 to 45 mL) water
¼ tsp (1 mL) garlic paste
¼ tsp (1 mL) salt
Chopped fresh chiles (optional)
12 corn tortillas (6 inches/15 cm) or tostada shells,
    (gluten-free if required)
1 Tbsp (15 ml) grapeseed or light vegetable oil
¾ cup (175 mL) shredded Gouda cheese
    or queso fresco (fresh Mexican cheese)
2½ cups (625 mL) shredded iceberg lettuce
¾ cup (175 mL) low-fat sour cream (gluten-free
    if required)
12 sprigs of cilantro (optional)

A day or two before you want to prepare this recipe, start the sprouts according to the recipe on page 5.

To make the salsa, combine the mango, tomatoes, diced red onion and cilantro in a medium bowl. In a small bowl, whisk together the lime juice, chipotle peppers, puréed garlic and salt. Pour over mango-tomato mixture and toss until evenly distributed.

To make the tostadas, mash the beans well and place in a small sauté pan or bowl. Stir in the minced red onion, water, garlic paste, salt and chiles (if using). Heat on medium-low or in the microwave until hot.

Preheat the oven to 450°F (230°C) with oven rack in the center position. Brush both sides of tortillas lightly with oil and place on a baking sheet (if using tostada shells, omit oil and heat until hot). Bake in the preheated oven for 5 minutes or until golden brown. Place hot tortillas on a large plate and cover partially with foil until ready to use.

When you're ready to serve, place a tortilla or tostada shell on a plate and spread evenly with 3 to 4 Tbsp (45 to 60 mL) of the bean mixture. Sprinkle with cheese, shredded lettuce, 2 to 3 Tbsp (30 to 45 mL) sprouts, salsa and sour cream. Garnish with cilantro if desired.

PER SERVING: Energy 470 calories; Protein 19 g; Carbohydrates 72 g; Dietary Fiber 11 g; Fat 12 g; Sugar 10 g; Cholesterol 30 mg; Sodium 360 mg

SAVORY SWEDISH MEATBALLS & GRAVY

MAKES 30 MEATBALLS (1¼ INCH/3 CM), SERVES 6

These meatballs are juicy, tender and enriched with sweet sorghum or oats. They are best served over the Kale & Cranberry Buckwheat Pilaf with Toasted Pecans & Thyme (page 102) but can be kept hot on the low setting in a slow cooker and served alone as an appetizer.

Mix together ¼ cup (60 mL) of the flour and the milk in a medium bowl. Let the mixture sit for 5 minutes. Add the beef, salt, allspice, nutmeg and ginger. Mix until thoroughly combined, then form into meatballs about 1¼ inches (3 cm) in diameter.

Preheat the oven to 350°F (180°C).

Heat a large saucepan on medium-high heat. Add the oil and brown the meatballs on all sides without fully cooking the inside. Place in an 8-cup (2 L) baking or casserole dish with a lid. Pour the beef broth over the balls. Cover with foil and the lid. Bake for 30 to 35 minutes, until the center is no longer pink. Pour the broth into the large saucepan.

In a small bowl, whisk together the remaining ¼ cup (60 mL) flour and ⅓ cup (75 mL) water. Heat the broth on medium-low. Whisk in the flour mixture and bring to a simmer. Stir until thickened, 2 to 3 minutes. Stir in the sour cream. Return the meatballs to the pot and serve when heated through. Or serve over the Kale & Cranberry Buckwheat Pilaf with Toasted Pecans & Thyme on page 102 if desired.

½ cup (125 mL) sorghum flour, divided
⅓ cup (75 mL) 1% milk
1 lb (450 g) extra-lean ground beef
½ tsp (2 mL) salt
½ tsp (2 mL) ground allspice
¼ tsp (1 mL) nutmeg
Pinch of ground ginger
1 Tbsp (15 mL) grapeseed or vegetable oil
3 cups (750 mL) low-sodium beef broth
⅓ cup (75 mL) water
¾ cup (175 mL) low-fat sour cream

PER SERVING (5 meatballs): Energy 220 calories; Protein 20 g; Carbohydrates 12 g; Dietary Fiber 1 g; Fat 10 g; Sugar 1 g; Cholesterol 50 mg; Sodium 300 mg.

As an option, use oat flour instead of sorghum flour.

SOUVLAKI AMARANTH MEATBALLS IN A PITA WITH CUCUMBER YOGURT DIP & FRESH VEGETABLES

MAKES 24 MEATBALLS, SERVES 4

The slightly sweet and nutty flavor of amaranth is delicious in a meatball paired with a cucumber yogurt dip, tomato and onion. Serve these meatballs inside a soft halved pita. For a delectable appetizer or small party snack, serve in mini pitas or as individual meatballs along with the dip.

MEATBALLS

1 cup (125 mL) water

⅓ cup (75 mL) amaranth seeds

1 lb (450 g) lean ground turkey
    or chicken

2 tsp (10 mL) lemon zest

2 Tbsp (30 mL) freshly squeezed
    lemon juice

2 tsp (10 mL) dried oregano

2 tsp (10 mL) garlic paste

½ tsp (2 mL) salt (optional)

Pinch of freshly ground
    black pepper

CUCUMBER YOGURT DIP

1 cup (250 mL) plain 2%
    Greek yogurt

½ cup (125 mL) packed grated
    English cucumber, squeezed
    of excess moisture

1 tsp (2 mL) garlic paste

¼ to ½ tsp (1 to 2 mL) salt

3 pita breads (whole wheat or
    gluten-free, if required), halved

1 cup (250 mL) chopped
    English cucumber

1 cup (250 mL) diced tomato

¼ cup (60 mL) thinly sliced
    red onion

Add the water and amaranth to a small saucepan and bring to a boil. Reduce to a simmer, cover and cook for 20 minutes. Remove from the heat and rinse amaranth with cold water in a fine-mesh strainer.

To make the dip, in a small bowl, mix the yogurt, grated cucumber, garlic and salt. Set aside.

Preheat the oven to 400°F (200°C). Place oven rack in the center position. Place a silicone mat or sheet of parchment on a large baking sheet and set aside.

To make the meatballs, combine the turkey, lemon zest, lemon juice, oregano, garlic, salt (if using), pepper and ¾ cup (175 mL) cooled amaranth. Use hands to mix evenly. Using a teaspoon, measure 2 teaspoons (10 mL) of mixture into the palm of your hand and roll into a ball. Place on the baking sheet at least 1½ inches (4 cm) apart. Repeat with the remaining mixture. Bake in preheated oven for 15 to 20 minutes, until meatballs are no longer pink. Broil for the last 2 to 3 minutes to slightly brown meatballs. Remove from the oven and immediately serve hot in a halved pita with chopped cucumber, tomato, red onion and Cucumber Yogurt Dip.

PER SERVING: Energy 360 calories; Protein 32 g; Carbohydrates 30 g; Dietary Fiber 4 g; Fat 14 g; Sugar 5 g; Cholesterol 80 mg; Sodium 510 mg.

APPLE CIDER-GLAZED PORK TENDERLOIN WITH BUTTERNUT SQUASH & SAGE ANCIENT GRAINS

SERVES 6

A warm and savory recipe with the rich autumn smells of brown butter, apple cider, butternut squash and sage. This is comfort food that is inviting, satisfying and truly nourishing.

For the tenderloin, preheat the oven to 350°F (180°C) with the oven rack in the center position.

Heat a Dutch oven or large saucepan on medium-high heat and add the oil. Sear all sides of both tenderloins and place in a small roasting pan. Roast in the preheated oven for 25 minutes or until an instant-read thermometer reads 170°F (80°C). Cover with foil and let rest for at least 8 minutes.

In a small saucepan, bring the apple cider to a simmer and reduce to ¾ cup (175 mL). Whisk together the stock and cornstarch in a small bowl; whisk into the apple cider and simmer on medium-low heat. Stir until the glaze has thickened and easily covers the back of a spoon, about 1 minute from the time it starts to simmer. Stir in vinegar, salt and white pepper. Set aside, covered.

For the grains, melt the butter in a large saucepan on medium heat, whisking constantly. Watch closely as brown flecks begin to appear. The butter will turn a caramel brown color and have a nutty fragrance. This step should take 4 to 6 minutes (if the butter turns black, start over). Remove browned butter from the heat immediately and use a spatula to move it all into a small bowl. Set aside.

Reheat the saucepan and add the oil. Stir in the onion and cook for about 7 minutes or until it starts to soften. Add the garlic and heat for 30 seconds. Stir in the chicken stock, millet and quinoa and bring to a boil. Reduce to a simmer and cook, covered, for 10 minutes. Place squash cubes across the top of the ancient grains (do not stir). Cover and simmer another 10 minutes or until the squash and grains are tender. Stir in the spinach until wilted. Toss with the brown butter and fresh sage. Season with salt if desired.

To serve, slice the pork loins into ½-inch (1 cm) thick slices. Lay pork over a bed of squash and sage ancient grains and drizzle glaze over the pork. Serve immediately.

PER SERVING: Energy 470 calories; Protein 41 g; Carbohydrates 41 g; Dietary Fiber 7 g; Fat 16 g; Sugar 3 g; Cholesterol 115 mg; Sodium 270 mg.

APPLE CIDER-GLAZED PORK TENDERLOIN

1 Tbsp (15 mL) grapeseed or vegetable oil

2 organic pork tenderloins (1 lb/450 g each)

1½ cups (375 mL) apple cider

1 cup (250 mL) chicken stock

2 tsp (10 mL) cornstarch

2 tsp (10 mL) apple cider vinegar

¼ tsp (1 mL) salt

Pinch of white pepper

BUTTERNUT SQUASH & SAGE ANCIENT GRAINS

3 Tbsp (45 mL) unsalted butter

1 Tbsp (15 mL) grapeseed oil

1 cup (250 mL) chopped onion

2 tsp (10 mL) minced garlic

3 cups (750 mL) chicken stock

½ cup (125 mL) millet seeds

½ cup (125 mL) quinoa seeds

1¼ to 1½ lb (565 to 675 g) butternut squash, peeled and cut into 1-inch (2.5 cm) cubes

4 cups (1 L) baby spinach

½ tsp (2 mL) minced fresh sage

Salt (optional)

ORANGE, GINGER & DIJON-GLAZED VEGETABLE & BUCKWHEAT SKILLET

SERVES 4

Tender-crisp veggies with a glaze of fresh orange juice, ginger and Dijon mixed with sirloin or your choice of meat, seafood or fried tofu on a bed of hot buckwheat. Adults and children alike will enjoy this exciting and nutritious dish.

3 cups (750 mL) water

1½ cups (375 mL) buckwheat groats

2 tsp (10 mL) freshly grated orange zest

1 cup (250 mL) freshly squeezed orange juice

1 Tbsp (15 mL) liquid honey or pure maple syrup

1 tsp (5 mL) mild Dijon mustard

1 tsp (5 mL) sriracha hot sauce or pinch of hot pepper flakes

2 Tbsp (30 mL) grapeseed or vegetable oil, divided

1 lb (450 g) beef sirloin tip, chicken or pork

4 cups (1 L) broccoli florets and pieces

2 cups (500 mL) thinly sliced carrots

1 red bell pepper, sliced

1 Tbsp (15 mL) puréed ginger

2 tsp (10 mL) minced garlic

¾ cup (175 mL) green onions, sliced diagonally

Tamari or soy sauce (optional)

In a large saucepan, bring the water and buckwheat to a boil. Reduce to a simmer, cover and cook for 15 minutes. Remove from the heat and drain off any liquid. Fluff with a fork and replace the cover.

Whisk together the orange zest, orange juice, honey, Dijon and sriracha sauce in a small bowl. Set aside.

Heat a large skillet or sauté pan with a lid on medium heat. Add 1 Tbsp (15 mL) oil and the sirloin or other meat you are using; cook on each side until desired doneness. Remove from the pan and set aside. Slice the meat after it has rested for 8 minutes.

Add the remaining tablespoon (15 mL) of oil to the skillet and reduce the heat to medium-low. Stir in the broccoli, carrots, red pepper, ginger and garlic. Cover and allow juices to collect in the pan. If the pan appears dry, add a tablespoon or two (15 to 30 mL) of water. Cook the vegetables for about 4 minutes, then pour in the orange juice mixture and replace lid until hot. Remove lid and stir in the sliced beef. Reduce sauce until slightly thickened and vegetables are crisp but tender. Sprinkle with green onion. Serve over warm buckwheat and encourage your family and guests to add tamari or soy sauce if they wish.

PER SERVING: Energy 360 calories; Protein 27 g; Carbohydrates 24 g; Dietary Fiber 5 g; Fat 17 g; Sugar 14 g; Cholesterol 75 mg; Sodium 160 mg.

- If you choose to use salmon instead, cook fillet by desired method until no longer pink and it flakes easily with a fork.
- Instead of buckwheat, you can use 3 cups (750 mL) of cooked kañiwa, quinoa, amaranth, teff or Superblend 1 or 2 (page 3).

OVEN-ROASTED HERB CHICKEN OVER TANGY APPLE & CABBAGE QUINOA

SERVES 6

Ancient grains, together with the fragrant aroma of herbed chicken, tart apples and crisp cabbage, make a well-rounded meal that is familiar, wholesome and so tasty.

Preheat the oven to 375°F (190°C). Dry the chicken with paper towels and place in a roasting pan. Divide the thyme and garlic into four parts and push under the skin to cover the breast and legs as evenly as you can (or put them into the cavity). Rub the skin with oil and season with salt. Roast, uncovered, for 15 minutes.

Reduce the temperature to 350°F (180°C). Cover and roast for an additional 30 minutes. Remove the lid and bake, uncovered, until the leg will move freely and the juices run clear, 15 to 18 minutes per pound. Remove from the oven, cover and keep warm.

To make the quinoa, heat a Dutch oven or large saucepan on medium-low heat. Add the oil and onion and cook, covered, for 5 to 7 minutes, until onions start to become tender. Stir in the stock, water and quinoa and bring to a boil. Reduce to a simmer and cook, covered, for 15 minutes. Lay the cabbage, apples, salt (if using) and pepper on top of the cooking quinoa (don't stir). Cover and cook for an additional 10 to 15 minutes or until the apples and cabbage are tender. Stir in the brown sugar and vinegar until sugar is dissolved and evenly distributed. Reseason with additional sugar and vinegar if desired. Remove skin and serve hot chicken over the quinoa with apples and cabbage.

PER SERVING: Energy 420 calories; Protein 52 g; Carbohydrates 25 g; Dietary Fiber 3 g; Fat 12 g; Sugar 11 g; Cholesterol 145 mg; Sodium 490 mg.

ROASTED HERB CHICKEN

1 roasting chicken (3 to 4 lb/1.5 to 2 kg), trussed
1 Tbsp (15 mL) fresh thyme or 1 tsp (5 mL) dried thyme
1 Tbsp (15 mL) minced garlic
1 Tbsp (15 mL) grapeseed or vegetable oil
½ tsp (2 mL) salt

TANGY APPLE & CABBAGE QUINOA

1 Tbsp (15 mL) grapeseed or vegetable oil
½ cup (125 mL) chopped yellow onion
1 cup (250 mL) low-sodium chicken stock
½ to ¾ cup (125 to 175 mL) water
½ cup (125 mL) quinoa seeds
4 cups (1 L) shredded red cabbage, ½ inch (1 cm) wide
2 Granny Smith apples, peeled, cored and sliced ¼ inch (5 mm) thick
½ tsp (2 mL) salt (optional)
Pinch of freshly ground black pepper
2 Tbsp (30 mL) brown sugar
2 Tbsp (30 mL) red wine vinegar

DESSERTS & BAKING

Once upon a time, our ancestors likely ate baking that was healthy. Why healthy? Because it was made with the natural wholesomeness of ancient grains untouched by modern-day processing. Today, we can enhance the overall goodness of sweet treats by bringing back these same grains and flours, which can provide so much nutrition. Chocolate Chip Chia Cookies (page 169) may sound too decadent to be healthy, but they're not! Replace traditional empty-calorie baking and desserts with dishes like Sorghum & Amaranth Sugar Cookies (page 178) or Maple Oat Bars (page 179) for delicious treats that will be kind to your body. Millet & Quinoa Blueberry Pecan Snack Bars (page 181) and Chocolate Chia Raisin Walnut Cookies (page 172) are terrific portable treats to take along in a lunch, as a snack or on a hike or a trip to the park. Impress your company—and good enough even to make for the kids—with Lemon & Blueberry Ancient Grain Pound Cake (page 186) and Ancient Grain Pumpkin Roll with Cream Cheese Filling (page 191).

MANGO RASPBERRY CHIA SORBET

MAKES 4 CUPS (1 L), SERVES 6

A smooth sorbet made with sweet mango, tangy raspberries and the gelling power of chia. Nutrition that is delicious, kid-friendly and oh so sneaky!

2 cups (500 mL) water
¼ cup (60 mL) white or organic cane sugar
⅔ cup (150 mL) ground white chia seeds
3 cups (750 mL) frozen mango chunks
1 cup (250 mL) frozen raspberries

Combine the water, sugar and chia in a blender and process until combined. Add frozen mango and raspberries and blend in batches until all fruit has been added. Continue to blend until smooth. Pour mixture into a shallow container and place in the freezer for 2 to 3 hours. (If container is too deep, sorbet will not freeze evenly.) Remove from freezer and scoop into serving dishes. Serve cold.

PER SERVING: Energy 190 calories; Protein 4 g; Carbohydrates 34 g; Dietary Fiber 10 g; Fat 6 g; Sugar 23 g; Cholesterol 0 mg; Sodium 5 mg.

> This dessert is best served fresh and not stored in the freezer.

CINNAMON SUGAR POPPED AMARANTH

MAKES 1 CUP (250 ML)

Popped amaranth or sorghum topped with cinnamon and sugar makes a tasty crunchy snack or topping for vanilla ice cream or any of your favorite desserts.

4 Tbsp (60 mL) amaranth seeds
1 Tbsp (15 mL) unsalted butter, melted
2 tsp (10 mL) white or organic cane sugar
¼ to ½ tsp (1 to 2 mL) cinnamon
Pinch of salt (optional)

Heat a dry 10- or 12-inch (25 or 30 cm) sauté pan with lid over medium heat for at least 1½ minutes. Place 1 Tbsp (15 mL) amaranth in the pan and cover quickly. Move pan from side to side on the burner. The seeds should start popping immediately. Remove pan from the heat when you can see that three-quarters of the amaranth has popped or when the popping begins to reduce. Keep lid on to pop any remaining seeds. Repeat with remaining 3 Tbsp (45 mL) amaranth. Place popped amaranth in a bowl and toss in the butter, sugar, cinnamon and salt (if using). Set aside to cool and dry completely.

PER SERVING: Energy 150 calories; Protein 3 g; Carbohydrates 18 g; Dietary Fiber 2 g; Fat 7 g; Sugar 2 g; Cholesterol 15 mg; Sodium 0 mg.

> Instead of amaranth, try sorghum grains.

CARAMEL APPLE BUCKWHEAT CRÊPES

MAKES 8 CRÊPES

Buckwheat flour makes a tasty and nutritious crêpe, and caramel and apples are the perfect sweet and fresh filling. This popular flavor combination was inspired by a little crêperie in the small town of Pezanas, in the south of France. You can also serve the crêpes topped with thick vanilla Greek yogurt, ice cream or whipped cream for a treat. If you're short on time, you can even make this recipe the night before. Gently reheat and build each crêpe.

CRÊPES

⅔ cup (175 mL) light buckwheat flour

2 tsp (10 mL) cornstarch

1 large egg

4 large egg whites

1 cup (250 mL) 1% milk

1 Tbsp (15 mL) pure maple syrup

Pinch of salt

CARAMELIZED APPLES

5 to 6 Fiji, pink lady or honey crisp apples, peeled, cored and cut into slices about ½ inch (1 cm) thick (about 2½ cups/625 mL)

3 Tbsp (45 mL) unsalted butter

¼ cup (60 mL) lightly packed brown sugar

½ tsp (2 mL) cinnamon

CARAMEL SAUCE

1 cup (250 mL) lightly packed brown sugar

2 Tbsp (30 mL) unsalted butter

½ cup (125 mL) table (18%) cream

Pinch of salt

Ice cream, whipped cream or thick vanilla Greek yogurt to serve (optional)

For the crêpes, stir the flour and cornstarch in a medium bowl. Whisk in the egg, egg whites, milk, maple syrup and salt until combined and smooth.

Heat a lightly oiled 6-inch (15 cm) crêpe pan or skillet on medium-high heat. Pour 3 Tbsp (45 mL) of batter into the center and tilt pan to move the batter in a circular motion to make a round crêpe. Flip when the edges begin to curl, about 30 to 45 seconds. Cook the other side of crêpe for another 30 seconds, place on a plate and cover with foil. Repeat with remaining batter. Set aside.

For the caramelized apples, prepare apples, then melt butter in a sauté pan over medium heat. Place apples in pan; sprinkle with the brown sugar and cinnamon. Cook, covered, until the sugar dissolves and apples are tender. Set aside to cool slightly (or completely, if desired).

For the caramel sauce, stir brown sugar into a saucepan over medium heat, stirring continuously until completely dissolved, about 3 minutes. Whisk in butter until melted and combined. Slowly pour in the cream, watching closely, as it can bubble over. Sprinkle in salt and stir to combine. Transfer to a glass container to cool slightly or completely before using.

To build the crêpes, lay one crêpe on a plate. Place about ½ cup (125 mL) of apples down the center, fold the crêpe over and drizzle 1 to 2 Tbsp (15 to 30 mL) of caramel sauce over each. Top with ice cream, whipped cream, or vanilla Greek yogurt (if using). Serve immediately.

PER SERVING (1 crêpe): Energy 250 calories; Protein 6 g; Carbohydrates 35 g; Dietary Fiber 2 g; Fat 10 g; Sugar 25 g; Cholesterol 50 mg; Sodium 135 mg.

MEXICAN CHOCOLATE MILLET PUDDING

SERVES 4

Millet is cooked, then blended into a rich and creamy chocolate pudding, spiced with cinnamon and the subtle, warm surprise of cayenne pepper.

1¼ cups (300 mL) water
½ cup (125 mL) millet seeds
¼ cup (60 mL) whole milk
⅓ cup (75 mL) white or organic cane sugar
3 Tbsp (45 mL) unsweetened cocoa powder
¼ tsp (1 mL) cinnamon
Pinch of cayenne pepper
Pinch of salt
Whipped cream (optional)

Combine the water and millet in a medium saucepan. Bring to a boil, then reduce to a simmer. Cover and simmer for 25 minutes. Remove lid and fluff with a fork. (If any water remains in the pot, simmer for a few minutes longer.) Set aside and allow to cool.

Place cooked millet, milk, sugar, cocoa, cinnamon, cayenne and salt in blender or food processor. Purée well, for at least 2 or 3 minutes, until smooth. Mixture should be very thick, but if it is not completely smooth or too thick, add a little more milk. Scoop into four serving dishes and chill for 1 hour or overnight before serving. Garnish with fresh whipped cream (if using) just before serving.

PER SERVING: Energy 170 calories; Protein 4 g; Carbohydrates 37 g; Dietary Fiber 5 g; Fat 2 g; Sugar 17 g; Cholesterol 0 mg; Sodium 80 mg.

> Instead of millet, use 1 cup (250 mL) of cooked quinoa, sorghum or amaranth.

RHUBARB PINEAPPLE AMARANTH PUDDING

SERVES 4

The tartness of rhubarb and the sweetness of pineapple make these two ingredients a wonderful pairing. Top this pudding with a large spoonful of creamy vanilla Greek yogurt to finish it off.

2½ cups (575 mL) water, divided
3 cups (750 mL) fresh or frozen rhubarb
1 can (14 oz/398 mL) unsweetened pineapple tidbits in juice
½ cup (125 mL) amaranth seeds
⅓ cup (75 mL) lightly packed brown sugar
5 tsp (25 mL) cornstarch

TOPPING

1 cup (250 mL) plain thick 1% Greek yogurt
1 Tbsp (15 mL) liquid honey or pure maple syrup
½ tsp (2 mL) pure vanilla extract

In a medium saucepan, combine 2 cups (500 mL) of the water, rhubarb, pineapple with juice, amaranth and brown sugar. Bring to a boil, then reduce to a simmer. Cover and simmer for 12 minutes. Stir and cook, covered, for 15 additional minutes, until amaranth is tender.

Whisk the cornstarch with the remaining ½ cup (125 mL) of water. Stir into the amaranth mixture, return to a simmer and cook for 1 minute, stirring constantly. Remove from the heat and divide among four bowls. Chill.

For the topping, stir the yogurt, honey and vanilla together in a small bowl. Divide among the chilled bowls of pudding and serve.

PER SERVING: Energy 310 calories; Protein 8 g; Carbohydrates 54 g; Dietary Fiber 4 g; Fat 8 g; Sugar 30 g; Cholesterol 10 mg; Sodium 35 mg.

CHOCOLATE CHIP CHIA COOKIES

MAKES 45 COOKIES

You would never know these soft, moist, chewy favorites are loaded with omega-3-rich chia and enriched with oats and millet. Make double batches and freeze for quick and easy snacks.

Combine chia and boiling water in a small bowl. Gently stir with a fork to ensure ground seeds are evenly distributed. Set aside to thicken.

Lightly grease or line a baking sheet with parchment. Preheat the oven to 375°F (190°C).

In a large bowl, cream the butter, chia mixture, brown sugar, white sugar, eggs and vanilla.

In a separate bowl, mix together the oats, millet flour, baking soda and salt. Add the butter mixture to the flour mixture and blend until well combined. Stir in the chocolate chips. Drop by rounded tablespoons (15 mL) 2 inches (5 cm) apart onto the prepared baking sheet.

Bake on the center rack of the preheated oven for 10 to 12 minutes. Remove from the oven and allow the cookies to cool for 5 minutes before moving to a wire rack to cool completely. Store the cookies in a sealed container in the refrigerator for up to 10 days.

- 2 Tbsp + 2 tsp (40 mL) ground chia seeds
- 3/4 cup (175 mL) boiling water
- 1/2 cup (125 mL) unsalted butter, softened
- 1/2 cup (125 mL) lightly packed brown sugar
- 1/2 cup (125 mL) white or organic cane sugar
- 2 large eggs
- 1 tsp (5 mL) pure vanilla extract
- 1¾ cups (425 mL) old-fashioned (large-flake) rolled oats
- 1 cup (250 mL) millet flour
- 1/2 tsp (2 mL) baking soda
- 1/2 tsp (2 mL) salt
- 1 cup (250 mL) semi-sweet chocolate chips

PER SERVING (1 cookie): Energy 80 calories; Protein 1 g; Carbohydrates 10 g; Dietary Fiber 1 g; Fat 3.5 g; Sugar 6 g; Cholesterol 15 mg; Sodium 45 mg.

ANCIENT GRAIN LEMON DROP COOKIES

MAKES 26 COOKIES

A powerhouse of nutritious, gluten-free flours makes a great flavor backdrop for these chewy, buttery lemon cookies. They're a perfect dose of tangy sweetness for all you lemon lovers!

1 cup (250 mL) quinoa flour
¼ cup (60 mL) amaranth flour
¼ cup (60 mL) sorghum flour
¼ cup (60 mL) coconut flour
1 tsp (5 mL) baking soda
½ cup (125 mL) unsalted butter, softened
½ cup (125 mL) white or organic cane sugar
¼ cup (60 mL) freshly grated lemon zest (approx. 2 lemons)
¼ cup (60 mL) freshly squeezed lemon juice
1 Tbsp (15 mL) unsweetened shredded coconut

Lightly grease or line a baking sheet with parchment. Preheat the oven to 350°F (180°C).

In a large bowl, mix together the quinoa, amaranth, sorghum and coconut flours. Mix in the baking soda and set aside.

In a separate bowl, cream the butter, sugar and lemon zest. Mix in the lemon juice. Pour the butter mixture into the flour mixture and beat until well combined. Roll teaspoons (5 mL) of dough in the coconut and place on the prepared baking sheet; gently flatten with the palm of your hand. (If dough is too sticky, place in the refrigerator for 15 to 20 minutes first.)

Bake on the center rack of the preheated oven for 10 to 12 minutes. Edges should just be starting to brown. Allow the cookies to cool for 10 minutes before moving to a wire rack to cool completely. Store the cookies in a sealed container in the refrigerator for up to 1 week.

PER SERVING (1 cookie): Energy 80 calories; Protein 1 g; Carbohydrates 9 g; Dietary Fiber 1 g; Fat 4.5 g; Sugar 4 g; Cholesterol 10 mg; Sodium 55 mg.

COCONUT CHOCOLATE QUINOA MACAROONS

MAKES 36 MACAROONS

These creamy coconut quinoa-flake cookies have a chewy center and are sweetened with chocolate—plus they taste as good as they look and are so easy to make!

Preheat the oven to 350°F (180°C). Ensure the rack is in the center position. Lightly spray or grease a large baking sheet and line with parchment or a silicone mat. Set aside.

Combine the coconut and quinoa flakes in a large bowl. In a medium bowl, whisk together the honey, egg whites and vanilla extract until combined. Pour over the coconut flake mixture and mix until uniform. Scoop the mixture by tablespoons (15 mL) onto the prepared baking sheet, keeping a 1-inch (2.5 cm) space between each. Use your fingers to mold each scoop into small mounds.

Bake in the preheated oven for 12 to 15 minutes. Remove when edges are golden and allow to cool for 30 minutes before removing from the pan.

Set up a double boiler and bring the water to a boil on medium-low heat. Place the chocolate in the top saucepan and stir until smooth and melted. Dip the bottom of each cookie in the chocolate and return to the parchment or silicone mat. Pour the remaining melted chocolate into a sealable plastic bag. Cut a ¼-inch (5 mm) tip off the end and pipe zig-zags of chocolate across each cookie. Cool and place in a sealable container, separating each layer with parchment or wax paper.

2 cups (500 mL) unsweetened shredded or flaked coconut

1 cup (250 mL) quinoa flakes

⅔ cup (150 mL) liquid honey

2 large egg whites

1 Tbsp (15 mL) pure vanilla or almond extract

⅔ cup (150 mL) semi-sweet or milk chocolate chips

PER SERVING (1 macaroon): Energy 80 calories; Protein 1 g; Carbohydrates 11 g; Dietary Fiber 1 g; Fat 4 g; Sugar 7 g; Cholesterol 0 mg; Sodium 35 mg.

> Try an equal amount of millet, amaranth or buckwheat flakes in place of the quinoa flakes.

CHOCOLATE CHIA RAISIN WALNUT COOKIES

MAKES 60 COOKIES

A deliciously soft fruit and nut cookie made with millet flour, quinoa flour and chia. Loaded with chocolate, raisins and walnuts, this recipe makes a big batch (thankfully).

2 Tbsp + 2 tsp (40 mL) ground chia seeds

¾ cup (175 mL) boiling water

½ cup (125 mL) unsalted butter, softened

1 cup (250 mL) lightly packed brown sugar

4 large eggs

2 tsp (10 mL) pure vanilla extract

⅓ cup (75 mL) raisins

1¼ cups (300 mL) quinoa flour

1¼ cups (300 mL) millet flour

2 tsp (10 mL) baking soda

½ tsp (2 mL) salt

⅓ cup (75 mL) semi-sweet chocolate chips

⅓ cup (75 mL) chopped walnuts

Combine chia and boiling water in a small bowl. Gently stir with a fork to ensure ground seeds are evenly distributed. Set aside to thicken.

Lightly grease or line a baking sheet with parchment. Preheat the oven to 375°F (190°C).

In a large bowl, cream the butter, chia mixture, brown sugar, eggs and vanilla. In a heatproof glass bowl or measuring cup, cover the raisins with 1 cup (250 mL) of boiling water and set them aside to rehydrate.

In a separate bowl, mix the quinoa flour, millet flour, baking soda and salt. Pour in the butter mixture and blend until well combined. Drain raisins and stir in along with the chocolate chips and walnuts. Drop by rounded tablespoons (15 mL) 2 inches (5 cm) apart onto the prepared baking sheet and flatten slightly with the palm of your hand.

Bake on the center rack of the preheated oven for 10 minutes. Allow the cookies to cool for 5 minutes before moving to a wire rack to cool completely. Store the cookies in a sealed container in the refrigerator for up to 10 days.

PER SERVING (1 cookie): Energy 60 calories; Protein 1 g; Carbohydrates 7 g; Dietary Fiber 1 g; Fat 3 g; Sugar 4 g; Cholesterol 15 mg; Sodium 70 mg.

- Instead of quinoa or millet flour, use sorghum flour or smaller portions of teff flour or light buckwheat flour.
- Try replacing the raisins with cranberries or dried cherries, or any combination of your favorites as an alternative.

Coconut Chocolate
Quinoa Macaroons

Sorghum & Amaranth
Sugar Cookies

Ancient Grain
Ginger Cookies

Chocolate Chip
Chia Cookies

ANCIENT GRAIN GINGER COOKIES

MAKES 30 COOKIES

This new take on an old favorite has the flavors of cinnamon, ginger and a hint of orange. The unconventional method of hydrating the flour before baking results in a gluten-free cookie that is chewy and healthy!

½ cup (125 mL) orange or
    apple juice
⅓ cup (75 mL) lightly packed
    brown sugar
¼ cup (60 mL) grapeseed
    or vegetable oil
¼ cup (60 mL) liquid honey
2 Tbsp (30 mL) fancy molasses
1 cup (250 mL) millet flour
1 cup (250 mL) oat flour
¼ tsp (1 mL) xanthan gum
2 tsp (10 mL) cinnamon
1 tsp (5 mL) ground ginger
½ tsp (2 mL) baking powder
¼ tsp (1 mL) salt
1 large egg white, beaten
3 Tbsp (45 mL) white or organic
    cane sugar

Whisk the orange juice, brown sugar, oil, honey and molasses in a sauté pan and bring to a simmer on medium-low heat. Stir in the millet and oat flours until the flour has absorbed the liquid. Remove from the heat and set aside to cool.

Combine the xanthan gum, cinnamon, ginger, baking powder and salt in a small bowl. Stir the egg white into the hydrated flour mixture. Add the dry ingredients and stir until completely incorporated. Place in a bowl and cover. Refrigerate for 2 hours or overnight.

Preheat the oven to 375°F (190°C) with a rack in the center position. Place parchment or a silicone mat on a baking sheet. Place the white sugar in a shallow bowl. Roll the dough into 1-inch (2.5 cm) balls. Roll balls of dough in the sugar and place 1½ inches (4 cm) apart on the baking sheet. Flatten to ½ inch (1 cm) with the palm of your hand.

Bake in the preheated oven for 9 to 10 minutes, until bottoms are golden. Cool on a wire rack and store in a sealed container in the refrigerator.

PER SERVING (1 cookie): Energy 70 calories; Protein 1 g; Carbohydrates 11 g; Dietary Fiber 1 g; Fat 2 g; Sugar 6 g; Cholesterol 0 mg; Sodium 25 mg.

CHOCOLATE CHIP & RAISIN OATMEAL SQUARES

MAKES 16 SQUARES

Chocolate, peanut butter and raisins are mixed with chia and oat flour. Slightly moist in the center, these yummy brownie-like squares contain no oil. Be sure not to overbake these morsels of goodness.

3 Tbsp (45 mL) chia seeds or ground chia seeds

¾ cup (250 mL) boiling water

½ cup (125 mL) natural peanut butter

⅓ cup (75 ml) liquid honey

⅓ cup (75 mL) lightly packed brown sugar

1 large egg

2 Tbsp (30 mL) water

½ cup (125 mL) oat flour

¼ cup (60 mL) sorghum flour

2 tsp (10 mL) baking powder

½ tsp (2 mL) baking soda

½ cup (125 mL) quick-cooking oats

½ cup (125 mL) raisins

⅓ cup (75 mL) milk chocolate chips

Combine chia and boiling water in a small bowl. Gently stir with a fork to ensure seeds are evenly distributed. Set aside to thicken.

Preheat the oven to 350°F (180°C) and lightly grease a 9-inch (2.5 L) square baking dish.

Combine the chia mixture, peanut butter, honey, brown sugar, egg and water in a small bowl. In a large bowl, whisk the oat flour, sorghum flour, baking powder and baking soda until well blended. Stir in the oats, raisins and chocolate chips. Stir in the wet ingredients until blended.

Pour batter into the prepared baking dish and bake for 28 to 30 minutes. Test for doneness (a toothpick inserted into the sides will come out clean but when inserted in the center will come out with a bit of moisture on it) and cool on a wire rack before cutting into squares. Refrigerate squares in a sealable container.

PER SERVING (1 square): Energy 150 calories; Protein 4 g; Carbohydrates 22 g; Dietary Fiber 2 g; Fat 6 g; Sugar 13 g; Cholesterol 10 mg; Sodium 80 mg.

> Instead of sorghum flour, use quinoa, millet or light buckwheat flour.

SORGHUM & AMARANTH SUGAR COOKIES

MAKES APPROXIMATELY 24 COOKIES, DEPENDING ON CUTTER SIZE

This light and fluffy, classic cut-out sugar cookie is just as you'd expect. Make all your favorite seasonal shapes with cookie cutters. Wonderful-tasting alone or ready to decorate with royal icing for any special occasion, this trouble-free dough is easy for kids to work with too!

Combine chia and boiling water in a small bowl. Gently stir with a fork to ensure ground seeds are evenly distributed. Set aside to thicken.

Lightly grease or line a baking sheet with parchment.

In a large bowl, cream the butter, chia mixture, sugar, eggs and vanilla. In a separate bowl, mix the quinoa, amaranth, sorghum and coconut flours. Mix in the baking powder and salt. Add the butter mixture to the flour mixture and mix until combined. Chill for 2 to 4 hours.

Preheat the oven to 350°F (180°C).

Roll out one-third of the dough on a floured surface to approximately ¼ inch (5 mm) thick. Using floured cutters, cut cookies into shapes and lift off with a metal cake lifter or spatula. Bake on the center rack of the preheated oven for 10 to 12 minutes. Edges should just be starting to brown. Allow the cookies to cool for 10 minutes before moving to a wire rack to cool completely. Decorate with your favourite frosting and colored sugar, if desired.

Store the cookies in a sealed container in the refrigerator for up to 10 days.

4 tsp (20 mL) ground white chia seeds

6 Tbsp (90 mL) boiling water

½ cup (125 mL) unsalted butter, softened

¾ cup (175 mL) white or organic cane sugar

2 large eggs

2 tsp (10 mL) pure vanilla extract

¾ cup (175 mL) quinoa flour

½ cup (125 mL) amaranth flour

½ cup (125 mL) sorghum flour

¾ cup (175 mL) coconut flour

1 tsp (5 mL) baking powder

½ tsp (2 mL) salt

PER SERVING (1 cookie): Energy 120 calories; Protein 2 g; Carbohydrates 15 g; Dietary Fiber 2 g; Fat 5 g; Sugar 6 g; Cholesterol 25 mg; Sodium 65 mg.

Make your own artisan cookies! Use a variety of cutters and natural food colors such as blackberry or beet juice. Add lavender, anise, lemon zest or seasoned sugar to customize your cookie cut-outs.

MAPLE OAT BARS

....

MAKES 25 BARS

Chia, quinoa and oats make this no-bake oat bar plain and simple. It is a buttery-tasting, maple-sweetened, portable snack for lunches or hikes, or a tea time treat worthy of the finest china.

Combine chia and boiling water in a small bowl. Gently stir with a fork to ensure ground seeds are evenly distributed. Set aside to thicken.

Grease or spray with cooking oil an 8-inch (2 L) square cake pan and line pan with parchment.

In a food processor or blender, grind the oats and quinoa flakes until they become a fine powder. In a large bowl, mix the ground oats, quinoa flakes, salt and cinnamon.

In a small saucepan on medium heat, melt the butter. Add the maple syrup and brown sugar. Heat until mixture is blended and sugar is dissolved. Remove from heat and allow to cool slightly. Mix in the chia mixture and vanilla. Pour syrup mixture over oat mixture; stir until well blended and mixture is moist and crumbly. Press into prepared pan with a spatula. Chill for 2 hours.

Cut into bars. Best served cold. Store the bars, separated by layers of wax paper or parchment, in a sealed container in the refrigerator for up to 10 days.

1 tsp (5 mL) ground white chia seeds

1½ Tbsp (22 mL) boiling water

2 cups (500 mL) rolled oats (old-fashioned or quick-cooking)

1 cup (250 mL) quinoa flakes

¼ tsp (1 mL) salt

1 tsp (5 mL) cinnamon

¼ cup (60 mL) unsalted butter

½ cup (125 mL) pure maple syrup

¼ cup (60 mL) lightly packed brown sugar

1 tsp (5 mL) pure vanilla extract

PER SERVING (1 bar): Energy 90 calories; Protein 2 g; Carbohydrates 16 g; Dietary Fiber 1 g; Fat 2.5 g; Sugar 5 g; Cholesterol 5 mg; Sodium 90 mg.

- Wrap individual bars and freeze for a quick portable snack.
- Instead of quinoa flakes, try millet, amaranth or buckwheat flakes, or any combination.

MILLET & QUINOA BLUEBERRY PECAN SNACK BARS

MAKES 16 BARS

Puffed millet and quinoa, along with chia and oats, are encased in a blanket of sweet honey and maple, spiced with cinnamon and nutmeg. The lively flavour of blueberries and the warmth of toasted pecans add hits of flavor and crunchy texture.

Grease or spray with cooking oil an 8-inch (2 L) square cake pan and line with parchment and set aside. Also line a rimmed baking sheet with parchment. Preheat the oven to 350°F (180°C).

Evenly spread the oats, pecans and chia seeds on the prepared baking sheet. Toast in the preheated oven for 5 to 6 minutes, until fragrant. Set aside to cool briefly.

In a large bowl, combine quinoa puffs, millet puffs and dried blueberries. Add the toasted pecans, oats and chia seeds. Stir and set aside.

In a medium saucepan, stir brown sugar, honey, maple syrup, butter and salt. Bring to a boil and reduce to a simmer. Cook until butter is melted and sugar is dissolved completely, 3 to 4 minutes. Remove from heat; stir in vanilla, cinnamon and nutmeg.

Pour syrup mixture over puff mixture. Stir until blended and mixture is evenly moistened. Press into pan with a spatula. Place an additional piece of parchment over the top and press firmly with your hands. Chill in the pan for 2 hours.

Lift and remove from pan and cut into bars. Best served cold. Store the bars, separated by layers of wax paper or parchment, in a sealed container in the refrigerator for up to 10 days.

PER SERVING (1 bar): Energy 190 calories; Protein 3 g; Carbohydrates 25 g; Dietary Fiber 4 g; Fat 9 g; Sugar 15 g; Cholesterol 10 mg; Sodium 40 mg.

1 cup (250 mL) old-fashioned (large-flake) rolled oats
1 cup (250 mL) chopped pecans
⅓ cup (75 mL) chia seeds
1 cup (250 mL) quinoa puffs
1 cup (250 mL) millet puffs
½ cup (125 mL) dried blueberries
½ cup (125 mL) lightly packed brown sugar
¼ cup (60 mL) liquid honey
¼ cup (60 mL) pure maple syrup
¼ cup (60 mL) unsalted butter
¼ tsp (1 mL) salt
2 tsp (10 mL) pure vanilla extract
½ tsp (2 mL) cinnamon
¼ tsp (1 mL) nutmeg

- Wrap individual bars and freeze for a quick, portable snack.
- Puffs used in this recipe can be all quinoa or all millet, amaranth, or any combination you choose.

PEANUT BUTTER CHIA BROWNIES

MAKES 16 SQUARES

These fudgy, moist brownies have a touch of creamy, nutty peanut butter. Full of a variety of ancient grains, they've got a good dose of protein, nutrients and hidden fiber. Nothing but goodness.

8 tsp (40 mL) ground chia seeds

¾ cup (175 mL) boiling water

1½ cups (375 mL) semi-sweet chocolate chips

½ cup (125 mL) white or organic cane sugar

2 large eggs

1 tsp (5 mL) pure vanilla extract

½ cup (125 mL) teff flour

½ cup (125 mL) sorghum flour

¼ cup (60 mL) kañiwa flour

½ tsp (2 mL) salt

¼ cup (60 mL) 1% milk

⅔ cup (150 mL) natural smooth peanut butter

¼ cup (60 mL) chopped peanuts

Combine chia and boiling water in a small bowl. Gently stir with a fork to ensure ground seeds are evenly distributed. Set aside to thicken.

Preheat the oven to 350°F (180°C). Spray or grease an 8-inch (2 L) square baking pan and line with parchment paper. Set aside.

In a small saucepan over low-medium heat, melt the chocolate chips. Stir until smooth and remove from the heat. Set aside to cool.

In a medium bowl, beat the sugar, chia mixture, eggs and vanilla. Add the melted chocolate and gradually add the teff flour, sorghum flour, kañiwa flour, salt and milk, mixing until well blended. Pour mixture into the prepared pan.

In a small saucepan over low heat, warm the peanut butter. Pour peanut butter over top of the brownie batter. Draw a knife through the peanut butter to streak it through the brownies evenly. Sprinkle with chopped peanuts.

Bake on the center oven rack for 25 to 30 minutes, until a toothpick inserted in the center comes out with only a few crumbs and edges are firm when pressed. Cool in the pan. Chill before cutting into 16 squares.

PER SERVING (1 square): Energy 230 calories; Protein 7 g; Carbohydrates 27 g; Dietary Fiber 3 g; Fat 12 g; Sugar 16 g; Cholesterol 25 mg; Sodium 135 mg.

You can use chunky peanut butter and leave out the chopped peanuts.

EAT MORE AMARANTH & CHIA SQUARES

MAKES 16 SQUARES

Fill the gap with energy and nutrition. Amaranth, sweet dates, peanut butter and cocoa make these chewy squares a must-have. Eat these squares when you need something to get you through to the next big meal. They make a handy snack before and after workouts.

Lightly grease a 9-inch (2.5 L) square baking dish, line with parchment and lightly grease parchment. Set aside.

Bring the water and amaranth to a boil in a small saucepan. Reduce to a simmer and cook, covered, for 20 minutes. Remove from the heat and let cool slightly (do not rinse amaranth).

Place the warm amaranth, dates, peanut butter, cocoa, oil and chia seeds in a food processor. Pulse and scrape down the sides until the dates are smooth and thoroughly mixed with the rest of the ingredients. Stir in the peanut pieces and spread into the baking dish. Cover and place in the fridge for 4 hours.

Cut into 16 pieces and store in a sealable container for up to 3 weeks.

1 cup (250 mL) water

⅓ cup (75 mL) amaranth seeds

1 cup (250 mL) dates

¾ cup (175 mL) smooth
    peanut butter

⅓ cup (75 mL) unsweetened
    cocoa powder

1 tsp (5 mL) toasted sesame oil

2 Tbsp (30 mL) chia seeds

1 cup (250 mL) chopped
    peanut pieces

PER SERVING (1 square): Energy 180 calories; Protein 6 g; Carbohydrates 16 g; Dietary Fiber 3 g; Fat 11 g; Sugar 8 g; Cholesterol 0 mg; Sodium 45 mg.

- No oat flour on hand? Remember, it's fast and easy to make homemade oat flour. See page 20.
- For variety, try making a batch of muffins with walnuts, pecans, or your favorite nut.

PINEAPPLE & CARROT ANCIENT GRAIN MUFFINS

MAKES 12

Pineapple and carrot with oats, sorghum and millet make a muffin with a load of flavor, texture and personality. Blending the flours together in a food processor along with the wet ingredients allows the liquid to be absorbed by the flour prior to baking, creating a more moist, less grainy muffin.

Place the oven rack in the center position and preheat the oven to 375°F (190°C). Fill a standard 12-cup muffin tin with paper liners.

Drain the juices well from the can of pineapple and measure out ⅔ cup (150 mL) of juice. Place the pineapple juice, oat flour, sorghum flour, millet flour, oil, brown sugar, eggs and vanilla in a blender or food processor and blend until smooth.

Combine the cinnamon, xanthan gum, baking powder, baking soda, salt and nutmeg until well blended.

Pour the liquid mixture into a large bowl. Sprinkle the cinnamon mixture over the batter. Mix together until just incorporated. Stir in the pineapple, carrot and raisins until just mixed.

Divide evenly among the muffin cups and bake for 18 to 20 minutes, until a toothpick inserted in the center comes out clean. Refrigerate muffins in a sealable container with the lid slightly cracked open.

PER SERVING (1 muffin): Energy 240 g calories; Protein 4 g; Carbohydrates 33 g; Dietary Fiber 4 g; Fat 11 g; Sugar 16 g; Cholesterol 30 mg; Sodium 180 mg.

1 can (14 oz/398 mL) crushed
   pineapple
1 cup (250 mL) oat flour
⅔ cup (150 mL) sorghum flour
⅔ cup (150 mL) millet flour
½ cup (125 mL) grapeseed or
   other light-tasting oil
¾ cup (175 mL) lightly packed
   brown sugar
2 large eggs
2 tsp (10 mL) pure vanilla extract
2 tsp (10 mL) cinnamon
1½ tsp (7 mL) xanthan gum
1½ tsp (7 mL) baking powder
½ tsp (2 mL) baking soda
½ tsp (2 mL) salt
¼ tsp (1 mL) nutmeg
1½ cups (375 mL) grated carrot
½ cup (125 mL) raisins

LEMON & BLUEBERRY ANCIENT GRAIN POUND CAKE

MAKES 1 LOAF, 12 SLICES

A combination of millet, sorghum, and light buckwheat flours along with chia seeds create this deliciously moist and tangy-sweet lemon pound cake that may taste rich but actually isn't.

1 Tbsp (15 mL) ground white
　chia seeds
4½ Tbsp (67 mL) boiling water
⅓ cup (75 mL) millet flour
⅓ cup (75 mL) light
　buckwheat flour
⅓ cup (75 mL) sorghum flour
¼ tsp (1 mL) baking powder
¼ tsp (1 mL) salt
⅓ cup (75 mL) unsalted butter
¾ cup (175 mL) white or organic
　cane sugar
2 large eggs
¼ cup (60 mL) lemon zest
⅓ cup (75 mL) freshly squeezed
　lemon juice
2 tsp (10 mL) pure vanilla extract
¾ cup (175 mL) fresh or frozen
　blueberries

Combine chia and boiling water in a small bowl. Gently stir with a fork to ensure ground seeds are evenly distributed. Set aside to thicken.

Grease or spray with cooking oil a 9- × 5-inch (2 L) loaf pan and line pan with parchment. Preheat the oven to 350°F (180°C).

In a large bowl, mix together the millet flour, buckwheat flour, sorghum flour, baking powder and salt; set aside.

In a separate bowl, cream the butter, chia mixture and sugar. Beat in the eggs, lemon zest, lemon juice and vanilla. Pour the butter mixture into the flour mixture and blend until well combined. Gently toss in blueberries. Scoop batter into loaf pan.

Bake on the center rack for 40 to 45 minutes, until a toothpick inserted in the center comes out clean. Edges should just be starting to brown. Remove from the oven and allow to cool for 5 minutes before moving to a wire rack to cool. Store in a sealed container in the refrigerator for up to 1 week.

PER SERVING (1 slice): Energy 150 calories; Protein 2 g; Carbohydrates 22 g; Dietary Fiber 2 g; Fat 6 g; Sugar 13 g; Cholesterol 45 mg; Sodium 60 mg.

> Use eggs that are at room temperature in baking recipes. This will achieve the most volume possible in your final baked goods.

WALNUT & BROWN SUGAR ANCIENT GRAIN BANANA LOAF

MAKES 1 LOAF, 8 SLICES

This moist and sweet banana bread, made with a combination of oat, sorghum and quinoa flour, is topped with a sprinkle of toasted walnuts and brown sugar.

⅓ cup (75 mL) oat flour
⅓ cup (75 mL) quinoa flour
⅓ cup (75 mL) sorghum flour
1 tsp (5 mL) baking soda
¼ tsp (1 mL) salt
1 large egg
2 large egg whites
⅓ cup (75 mL) unsweetened
    applesauce
¼ tsp (1 mL) grapeseed oil
⅓ cup (75 mL) lightly packed
    brown sugar
1 cup (250 mL) mashed ripe
    banana

TOPPING
3 Tbsp (45 mL) chopped walnuts
2 Tbsp (30 mL) brown sugar
1 tsp (5 mL) unsalted butter

Preheat the oven to 350°F (180°C) and adjust the oven rack to center position. Lightly grease a 9- × 5-inch (2 L) loaf pan and line the two sides and the bottom with one piece of parchment. Lightly grease parchment and set aside.

Whisk together the oat flour, quinoa flour, sorghum flour, baking soda and salt in a small bowl. Set aside.

Whisk together the egg, egg whites, applesauce, oil, brown sugar and banana in a medium bowl. Gently stir the dry ingredients into the wet until almost mixed.

To make the topping, mix together the chopped walnuts, brown sugar and butter with clean hands in a small bowl.

Pour batter into the prepared loaf pan and sprinkle the topping across the top. Bake for 45 minutes or until a toothpick inserted into the center comes out clean. Cool slightly before lifting the loaf out of the pan. Cool on a wire rack. Slice while still warm or completely cooled.

PER SERVING (1 slice): Energy 150 calories; Protein 4 g; Carbohydrates 26 g; Dietary Fiber 3 g; Fat 4 g; Sugar 13 g; Cholesterol 25 mg; Sodium 260 mg.

DOUBLE CHOCOLATE ANCIENT GRAIN BANANA LOAF

MAKES 1 LOAF, 8 SLICES

Sorghum and quinoa or oat flour make this double chocolate treat healthy and indulgent at the same time. Make 2 loaves and freeze one for another time if desired.

Preheat the oven to 350°F (180°C) and adjust the oven rack to center position. Lightly grease a 9- × 5-inch (2 L) loaf pan and line the two sides and the bottom with one piece of parchment. Lightly grease parchment and set aside.

Whisk together the quinoa flour, sorghum flour, cocoa, baking soda and salt in a small bowl, making sure lumps are out of the cocoa.

Whisk together the egg, egg whites, applesauce, oil, brown sugar and banana in a medium bowl. Gently stir the dry ingredients into the wet until almost mixed. Stir in the chocolate chips until evenly distributed. Pour batter into the loaf pan and bake for 45 minutes or until a toothpick inserted into the center comes out clean.

Cool slightly before lifting the loaf out of the pan. Cool on a wire rack. Slice while still warm or completely cooled.

Per Serving (1 slice): Energy 240 calories; Protein 5 g; Carbohydrates 33 g; Dietary Fiber 4 g; Fat 12 g; Sugar 16 g; Cholesterol 25 mg; Sodium 260 mg.

½ cup (125 mL) quinoa or oat flour

½ cup (125 mL) sorghum flour

¼ cup (60 mL) unsweetened cocoa powder

1 tsp (5 mL) baking soda

¼ tsp (1 mL) salt

1 large egg

2 large egg whites

⅓ cup (75 mL) unsweetened applesauce

¼ cup (60 mL) grapeseed or vegetable oil

⅓ cup (75 mL) lightly packed brown sugar

1 cup (250 mL) mashed ripe banana

½ cup (125 mL) semi-sweet chocolate chips

ANCIENT GRAIN PUMPKIN ROLL WITH CREAM CHEESE FILLING

SERVES 8

A wonderful pumpkin spice roulade made with millet, sorghum and oat flour, with a creamy, smooth filling that makes a slice of this a delicious tea-time treat or formal dessert.

Preheat the oven to 350°F (180°C). Grease and line with parchment a 17¼- × 11½-inch (42 × 29 cm) rimmed baking sheet. Lightly spray with cooking oil or grease the parchment also. Set aside.

In a large bowl, whisk the flours, cinnamon, xanthan gum, baking powder, ground ginger and salt until blended. In a medium bowl, whisk the brown sugar, eggs, egg whites and pumpkin until blended and no lumps remain. Pour the pumpkin mixture into the dry ingredients and mix until combined. Spread the dough in two-thirds of the pan only, about ½ inch (1 cm) thick. Sprinkle evenly with walnuts. Bake for 11 to 12 minutes, until the edges are golden and an inserted toothpick comes out clean. Remove from the oven and place the pan on a wire rack to cool until warm (if cake is hot when rolled, it will be too moist and crack).

Remove pan from the rack and place a clean dish towel over the entire cake with about 2 inches (5 cm) hanging over one end. Place the cooling rack over top of towel. Flip the pan over onto the cooling rack and towel. Take the edge of the towel hanging over the end and fold it over one end of the cake. Gently roll the cake loosely into a log and cool completely (minimum 1 hour or overnight).

Make the filling by whisking the milk, brown sugar and cornstarch in a small saucepan on medium-low heat, whisking constantly. Mixture will thicken about 1 minute after starting to bubble. Break the cream cheese into the pot and stir until melted and fully incorporated. Place a piece of parchment or wax paper directly on top of the surface of the filling and allow to cool completely.

Gently unroll the cake, spread with filling and roll back up into a log. Cover with plastic wrap and chill in the refrigerator for 3 hours or more. Trim both ends, score into 8 pieces and slice when ready to serve.

PER SERVING (1 slice): Energy 250 calories; Protein 11 g; Carbohydrates 31 g; Dietary Fiber 4 g; Fat 10 g; Sugar 14 g; Cholesterol 65 mg; Sodium 300 mg.

⅓ cup (75 mL) sorghum flour
⅓ cup (75 mL) millet flour
⅓ cup (75 mL) oat flour
2 tsp (10 mL) cinnamon
2½ tsp (12 mL) xanthan gum
¾ tsp (3 mL) baking powder
¾ tsp (3 mL) ground ginger
½ tsp (2 mL) salt
1¼ cups (300 mL) lightly packed
    brown sugar
2 large eggs
2 large egg whites
1 cup (250 mL) pumpkin purée
⅓ cup (75 mL) chopped walnuts

FILLING

1½ cups (375 mL) 1% milk
½ cup (125 mL) lightly packed
    brown sugar
3 Tbsp (45 mL) cornstarch
1 package (8 oz/250 g) low-fat
    cream cheese

CHOCOLATE ANCIENT GRAIN TORTE WITH RASPBERRY CHIA SAUCE

SERVES 6

Dessert powered with omega-3 nutrition, protein and plenty of vitamins and minerals. Sorghum provides the base for this rich chocolate torte. Top it with the raspberry chia sauce for a soul-satisfying dessert.

3¾ cups (925 mL) water

1¼ cups (300 mL) sorghum grains

⅓ cup (75 mL) unsalted butter, melted

1 large egg

3 large egg whites

¾ cup (175 mL) lightly packed brown sugar

½ cup + 2 Tbsp (155 mL) sifted unsweetened cocoa powder

2 tsp (10 mL) pure vanilla extract

¼ tsp (1 mL) salt

RASPBERRY CHIA SAUCE

1 cup (250 mL) fresh or frozen raspberries

¼ cup (60 mL) white or organic cane sugar

1 Tbsp (15 mL) chia seeds

Bring the water and sorghum to a boil in a medium saucepan. Reduce to a simmer and cook, covered, for 60 minutes. Remove from the heat, drain, then cool (the sorghum should be very tender).

Lightly grease a 9-inch (23 cm) springform pan. Cut a piece of parchment to fit the bottom and lightly grease the parchment. Preheat the oven to 350°F (180°C) with the rack in the center position.

Place 3 cups (750 mL) of the cooled sorghum, melted butter, egg, egg whites, and brown sugar in a blender. Purée until smooth and no large pieces remain. Transfer batter to a medium bowl and whisk in cocoa, vanilla and salt. Pour batter into the prepared pan and bake for 40 minutes, until the center is no longer liquid but still moist. Cool the torte for 2 hours.

To make the sauce, mash the raspberries with the back of a fork in a shallow bowl. Stir in the sugar and chia. Let set for 30 minutes in the refrigerator.

Cut torte into desired servings and serve with chilled Raspberry Chia Sauce.

PER SERVING: Energy 390 calories; Protein 10 g; Carbohydrates 65 g; Dietary Fiber 8 g; Fat 14 g; Sugar 27 g; Cholesterol 60 mg; Sodium 150 mg.

> This torte is also terrific with 1½ cups (375 mL) each of fluffy cooked millet and quinoa in place of the sorghum.

RUSTIC ALMOND & OAT PEAR TART

SERVES 6

Warm and tender baked pears framed in a casual almond-oat crust is scrumptious, especially when topped with a small scoop of vanilla ice cream. An easy, no-fuss dessert that is rustic, charming and good for you.

Preheat the oven to 375°F (190°C) and place a piece of parchment or a silicone mat on a large baking sheet.

Whisk the oat flour, almond flour, xanthan gum, baking powder and salt in a medium bowl until evenly distributed. Whisk in the brown sugar, breaking up any lumps. Cut in cold butter with a pastry cutter (or grate from semi-frozen) until butter is pea-sized. Gently fold in milk and almond extract (if using) until dough sticks together. Form into a disk, wrap with plastic wrap and refrigerate for 1 hour.

Preheat the oven to 400°F (200°C) with the oven rack in the center position. Tear or cut a piece of parchment to line a baking sheet.

Remove the parchment from the pan and sprinkle with flour. Place dough on parchment and roll into a circle about 12 inches (30 cm) in diameter and about ¼ inch (5 mm) thick, lifting frequently to make sure it's not sticking. Sprinkle a small amount of flour under the dough if it sticks. Place parchment and rolled pastry back onto the baking sheet by grabbing diagonal corners of the parchment and lifting to the baking sheet.

To make the filling, gently toss the pears, lemon zest, brown sugar, cornstarch and cinnamon. Place the pear mixture in the center of the crust and spread to 1½ inches (4 cm) from the edge. Fold over the edge all around, flattening the pear filling slightly into the tart and folding the crevices. Sprinkle with a few sliced almonds if desired.

Bake for 20 to 25 minutes, until the pears are tender and the crust is golden. Remove from the oven and cool slightly before cutting into portions and serving with ice cream, if using.

PER SERVING: Energy 250 calories; Protein 4 g; Carbohydrates 34 g; Dietary Fiber 6 g; Fat 13 g; Sugar 20 g; Cholesterol 20 mg; Sodium 110 mg.

CRUST

½ cup (125 mL) finely ground oat flour
½ cup (125 mL) finely ground almond flour
2 tsp (5 mL) xanthan gum
¼ tsp (1 mL) baking powder
¼ tsp (1 mL) salt
2 Tbsp (30 mL) brown sugar
¼ cup (60 mL) cold butter
1 Tbsp (15 mL) milk or milk substitute
¼ tsp (1 mL) pure almond extract (optional)
Light flour for dusting, such as rice or sorghum

FILLING

3 firm ripe pears, cored and cut into ¼-inch (5 mm) thick slices and tossed in 1 Tbsp (15 mL) freshly squeezed lemon juice
1 tsp (5 mL) lemon zest
¼ cup (60 mL) lightly packed brown sugar
1 Tbsp (15 mL) cornstarch
¼ tsp (1 mL) cinnamon
1 tsp (5 mL) sliced almonds (optional)
Vanilla ice cream (optional)

TROUBLESHOOTING TIPS & TRICKS

Excess water in the saucepan after cooking grains

Sometimes, grains or seeds cook this way. Most of the time, the easy fix is to extend the cooking time. If the water is still warm, just cover the saucepan and let it sit for some additional time, until you can lift the lid and see that no water is remaining and the grains/seeds are cooked. If the saucepan has cooled, bring the mixture to a boil and then turn off the heat and leave it for another few minutes. Check to see that the water has absorbed. If there is still water in the saucepan but the grains are cooked to your liking, simply drain any excess water from the saucepan.

Adding grains to recipes—cooked or raw?

Most of the time, grains are added raw, unless it is specified in the recipe that they are precooked. The recipe should have sufficient liquid and cooking time to allow for the uncooked grains to cook and expand.

Soaking grains prior to cooking

Some people prefer to soak grains or seeds prior to cooking to break them down a bit first. This is an alternative for raw food eaters, it can speed cooking times, and some claim it may even help with digestion.

Raw food diets and ancient grains

Yes, raw foodies can eat ancient grains! Most ancient grains and seeds can be sprouted or grown. Mucilaginous seeds such as chia need to be grown as microgreens, grown in soil or on a felt pad, as they produce too much gel if you try to sprout them in water. Other seeds and grains, such as kañiwa, quinoa, millet, buckwheat and even teff, should be sprouted, regardless of mucilaginous properties.

Cooking in the microwave oven

We don't recommend reheating or cooking grains and seeds in a microwave oven. It doesn't provide the best end result, nor does it consistently provide the same result. Keep in mind that microwave ovens are suspected to contribute to ill health, as they significantly deplete or modify nutrients in food and may even create cancer-causing free radicals.

Overcooked ancient grains

Don't throw them away! Overcooked grains can be used in many recipes, such as breakfast cereals, in scrambled eggs, or added to meatloaves, burgers, smoothies and even muffin batters. Examples include our Chocolate Banana & Peanut Butter Amaranth Smoothie (page 34), Prosciutto & Kale Kañiwa Frittata with Romano Cheese (page 65), Cheddar Cauliflower Amaranth Soup with

Sherry & Thyme, Souvlaki Amaranth Meatballs with Cucumber Yogurt Dip & Fresh Vegetables (page 154) and Savory Swedish Meatballs & Gravy (page 153).

Freezing cooked ancient grains
Can you freeze leftover cooked ancient grains? Yes, you can! We even recommend freezing pre-cooked grains in cooled, premeasured amounts for up to 1 month because this makes for easy meal preparation. Just heat and serve!

Rice cookers and steamers
Yes, you can cook ancient grains in rice cookers or steamers. There are many different models out there, so we suggest experimenting with yours.

Xanthan gum and guar gum
This book uses xanthan gum in several recipes. Simply to be consistent, we chose to work with xanthan gum. It is the best for baking and those are the recipes in which we generally used it. Alternatively, you can experiment with using guar gum as per the instructions on the package. Read more about gluten-free cooking with xanthan gum and guar gum on page xix.

Where to buy ancient grains?
Ancient grains can be found in most major supermarkets worldwide, sometimes found in the organic or specialty sections of the store. They can also be purchased at bulk food, health food and specialty food stores as well as online.

Are all ancient grains gluten-free?
No. However, in this book we have chosen to specifically use ancient grains that are gluten-free.

They are amaranth, buckwheat, chia, kañiwa, millet, oats, quinoa, sorghum and teff.

I'm new to ancient grains, where should I start?
If you're new to cooking with ancient grains, we certainly recommend you read the Basics chapter of this book to become more familiar with what you'd like to start with. Good starter recipes are breakfast cereals or easy soups or salads.

Why use flour blends? Can you just use one type of flour in a recipe instead of the two or three listed?
Blends of flours are used to create the most likable flavor, texture and nutrition. Especially important where gluten is absent, blending various gluten-free flours and combining their various properties is critical to getting a positive end result.

Taste differences in ancient grains
If you don't like the taste or texture of a particular ancient grain, you will notice we make suggestions for other alternatives in most recipes. Also, we encourage you to experiment or try using a Superblend (see Basics chapter, page 3).

Organic, non-GMO and fair trade
Are all ancient grains organic, non-GMO and fair trade? We recommend that if you are concerned about buying certified organic, non-GMO and fair trade products that you only buy products specifically labeled as such. With the renewed success of ancient grains in the market, new brands and products are on store shelves every day and competition is fierce. Buy what is properly labeled, stamped and certified.

RESOURCES

www.patriciaandcarolyn.com
Information on cooking quinoa and other ancient grains, and on our cookbooks.

www.wholegrainscouncil.org
A useful site for definitions and valuable information on all grains.

www.chia.org.uk
Includes history and other information on chia.

www.ars.usda.gov/Services/docs.htm?docid-8964
USDA National Nutrient Database for Standard Reference, 2012.

www.bobsredmill.com
Gluten-free resources, product information and a large range of high-quality ancient grains and gluten-free ingredients.

www.andeannaturals.com
Expert information on non-GMO, certified organic and fair trade certified quinoa and kañiwa seeds, flour, puffs, crisps, germ and flakes.

www.celiac.com
Celiac disease and gluten-free diet information.

www.edisongrainery.com
A variety of high quality, certified organic, gluten-free ingredients including seeds, grains, flours, flakes, puffs, crisps and more.

www.alterecofoods.com
An organization of fair-trade product experts, specializing in the import and distribution of fair-trade products including quinoa and chocolate.

REFERENCES

"Ancient Grains Encourage Biological Diversity." 1991. Montreal: Ecological Agriculture Projects, McGill University. Retrieved Sept. 6, 2012, at http://eap.mcgill.ca/CPC_2.htm.

Anderson, G.H., Cho, C.E., Akhavan, T., Mollard, R.C., Luhovyy, B.L., & Finocchiaro, E.T. 2010. "Relation between Estimates of Cornstarch Digestibility by the Englyst In Vitro Method and Glycemic Response, Subjective Appetite, and Short-Term Food Intake in Young Men." *American Journal of Clinical Nutrition* 91(4): 932–39.

Arguedas Gamboa, P. 2008. "Teff: Survey on the Nutritional Health Aspects of *Eragrostis tef*." *Cartago: Instituto Tenológico de Costa Rica*: 353–59.

Beck, E., Tapsell, L., Batterham, M., Tosh, S., & Huang, X. 2009. "Increases in Peptide Y-Y Levels Following Oat Beta Glucan Ingestion." *Nutrition Research* 10: 705–09.

Beck, Leslie. 2011. "What's the Healthiest Cooking Oil?" *Globe and Mail*, Feb. 16.

Bressani, R. 1989. "The Proteins of Grain Amaranth." *Food Reviews International* 5: 13–88.

Bressani, R., Elias, L., & Garcia-Soto, A. 1989. "Limiting Amino Acids in Raw and Processed Amaranth Grain Protein from Biological Tests." *Plant Foods for Human Nutrition* 39(3): 2

Cade, J.E., Burley, V.J., & Greenwood, D.C. 2007. "Dietary Fibre and Risk of Breast Cancer in the UK Women's Cohort Study." *International Journal of Epidemiology* 36(2): 431–38.

Chung, O.K., Bean, S.R., & Park, S.H. 2005. "Sorghum Foods: New Health Benefits from an Ancient Grain." *Food Science Journal* (Chinese) 25: 431–37.

Dae Won, K., et al. 2009. "Germinated Buckwheat Extract Decreases Blood Pressure and Nitrotyrosine Immunoreactivity in Aortic Endothelial Cells." *Phytotherapy Research* 23(7): 993–98.

Djousse, L., & Gaziano, J. 2007. "Breakfast Cereals and Risk of Heart Failure in the Physicians' Health Study I." *Archives of Internal Medicine* 167(19): 2080–85.

Eskin, M. 2002. *Quinoa: Properties and Performance*. Kamsack, SK: Shaw, 5–12.

Farrar, J., Hartle, D., Hargrove, J., & Greenspan, P. 2008. "A Novel Nutraceutical Property of Select Sorghum Bran." *Phytotherapy Research* 22(8): 1052–56.

Gomez-Cordoves, C., Bartolome, B., Viera, W., & Virador, V. 2001. "Effects of Wine Phenolics and Sorghum Tannins on Tyrosinase Activity and Growth of Melanoma Cells." *Journal of Agricultural and Food Chemistry* 49(3): 1620–24.

Green, P., & Hemming, C. 2012. "Introduction — Revolutionizing Health and Fitness with Quinoa." *Quinoa Revolution*: xiii.

Lammert, A., et al. 2008. "Clinical Benefit of Short-Term Dietary Oatmeal Intervention in Patients with Type 2 Diabetes and Severe Insulin Resistance." *Experimental and Clinical Endocrinology and Diabetes* 116(2): 132–34.

Lee, S., Chung, I., Cha, Y., & Park, Y. 2010. "Millet Consumption Decreased Serum Concentration of Triglyceride and C-Reactive Protein." *Nutrition Research* 30(4): 290–96.

Maki, K., et al. 2007. "Effects of Consuming Foods Containing Oat Beta Glucan on Blood Pressure, Carbohydrate Metabolism and Oxidative Stress in Men and Women with Elevated Blood Pressures." *European Journal of Clinical Nutrition* 61(6): 786–95.

Marcone, M., Kakuda, Y., & Yada, R. 2003. "Amaranth as a Rich Dietary Source of Beta-Sitosterol and Other Phytosterols." *Plant Foods for Human Nutrition* 58(3): 207–11.

Mason, R. 2001. *What Is Beta Glucan?* Sheffield, MA: Safe Goods Publishing.

Nicol, B.M., & Philips, P.G. 1978. "The Utilization of Proteins and Amino Acids in Diets Based on Cassava, Rice or Sorghum. *British Journal of Nutrition* 39: 271–87.

Nuñez de Arco, S. 2012. "Organic Quinoa and Quinoa-based Ingredients Information." Andean Naturals, Inc.

Panasiuk, O., & Bills, D.D. 1984. "Cyanide Content of Sorghum Sprouts." *Journal of Food Science* 49: 791–93.

Pirello, C. 2010. "Change Your Life with Chia." *Huffington Post*. Retrieved Nov. 21, 2012, at www.huffingtonpost.com/christina-pirello/change-your-life-with-chi_b_446413.html.

Platel, K., Elpeson, S., & Srinivasan, K. 2010. "Bioaccessible Mineral Content of Malted Finger Millet, Wheat and Barley." *Journal of Agricultural and Food Chemistry* 58(11): 6706–14.

Prestano, G., Pedrazuela, A., Penas, E., Lasuncion, M., & Arroyo, G. 2003. "Role of Buckwheat Diet on Rats as Prebiotic and Healthy Food." *Nutrition Research* 23(6): 803–14.

Qureshi, A., Lehmann, J., & Peterson, D. 1966. "Amaranth and Its Oil Inhibit Cholesterol Biosynthesis." *Journal of Nutrition* 126(8): 1972–78.

Repo-Carrasco, R., Espinoza, C., & Jacobsen, S.E. 2003. "Nutritional Value and Use of the Andean Crops Quinoa (*Chenopodium quinoa*) and Kañiwa (*Chenopodium pallidicaule*)." *Food Reviews International* 19(1–2): 179–89.

Rondanelli, M., Opizzi, A., & Monteferrario, F. 2009. "The Biological Activity of Beta Glucans." *Minerva Medica* 100(3): 237–45.

Scheppach, W. 1994. "Effects of Short-Chain Fatty Acids on Gut Morphology and Function." *GUT: An International Journal of Gastroenterology and Hepatology* 35(1): 35–38.

Silva-Sanchez, C., et al. 2008. "Bioactive Peptides in Amaranth Seed." *Journal of Agricultural and Food Chemistry* 56(4): 1233–40.

Sireesha, Y., Kasetti, R.B., Nabi, S.A., Sirasanagandia, S., & Apparao, C. 2011. "Antihyperglycemic and Hypolipidemic Activities of *Setaria italica* Seeds in STZ Diabetic Rats." *Pathohysiology* 18(2): 159–64.

Skrabanja, V., Liljeberg Elmstahl, H., Kreft, I., & Bjork, I. 2001. "Nutritional Properties in the Starch of Buckwheat Products." *Journal of Agricultural and Food Chemistry* 49(1): 490–96.

Stokes, A. 2008. "The Chia Cheat Sheet." Retrieved Nov. 7, 2012, at www.naturalnews.com/022468_chia_seeds_food.html.

Tsai, C.J., Leitzmann, M.F., Willett, W.C., & Giovanucci, E.L. 2004. "Long-Term Intake of Dietary Fiber and Decreased Risk of Cholecystectomy in Women." *American Journal of Gastroenterology* 99(7): 1364–70.

van Dam, R.M., Hu, F.B., Rosenberg, L., Krishnan, J., & Palmer, J.R. 2006. "Dietary Calcium and Magnesium, Major Food Sources, and Risk of Type 2 Diabetes in U.S. Black Women." *Diabetes Care* 29(10): 2238–43.

Virtanen, S., et al. 2010. "Early Introduction of Oats Associated with Decreased Risk of Persistent Asthma and Early Introduction of Fish with Decreased Risk of Allergic Rhinitis." *British Journal of Nutrition* 103(2): 266–73.

Wright, C. 2012. "Tame Hunger and Cravings with Serotonin." *Natural News*. Retrieved Nov. 27, 2012, at www.naturalnews.com/037256_hunger_cravings_serotonin_appetite.html.

Xiao, Z., Lester, G.E., Luo, Y. & Wang Q. 2012. "Assessment of Vitamin and Carotenoid Concentrations of Emerging Food Products: Edible Microgreens." *Journal of Agricultural and Food Chemistry* 60(31): 7644–51.

Yang, L., Browning, J., & Awika, J. 2009. "Sorghum 3-Deoxyanthocyanins Possess Strong Phase II Enzyme Inducer Activity and Cancer Cell Growth Inhibition Properties." *Journal of Agricultural and Food Chemistry* 57(5): 1797–804.

ACKNOWLEDGMENTS

To Paul and Ian, and always amazing, our Aston, Alyssa and Sydney. Also Vera Friesen, Swen Runkvist and Bill & Val Green. We are always grateful for the support of numerous industry advisors, scientists, growers, supporters, friends and family. Sergio & Lisa Nuñez de Arco, Marcos Guevara, Laurie Scanlin & Claire Burnett, Jeffrey & Amy Barnes, the folks at Specialty Commodity, Marjorie & Bob Leventry, Francisco & Magdalena Diez-Canseco, Bob Moore, Nancy, Sarah and the entire Bob's Red Mill team, Olivier & Didier Perreol, Gordon Kirke, Chuck Watson, Alpha Harper, Ole Runkvist, Shelley Runkvist & family, Kathy Holford, Terri Regan, Petra & Victor Arp and the entire Arp clan, Shawn & Alex Taylor, Dr. Stephanie Anisko, Leslie Edmunds, Annette Shute, Janine Kemp, Allie & Tammy Grieco, Frank Dyson, Rachel Cambell, Ken & Noreen McLean, Sheila, Mark & Jess Gordon, Sara Busby, Kerri Rosenbaum Barr, Billijon Morgan, Sandy Wasylyniuk & family, Tara & Jake Trottier, Annette Collins, Treena Klagenberg & Rob Person, Chris Bingham, Dallas Waldner, Bobbi & Ashley Beuker, Kate Blake & Jay Currier, Marg & Tony Blake, Joanne Fleet & Jeff Blake, Katherine, Joe & Kate Keresztesi, Heather Nusl, Ian & Mia Kruger, Verna Deason and the Deason family, Uncle John & Aunt Beryl, John, Heather & Ella Barber, Dave, Sue, Baylea and Sam Barber, and Gary & Karen Barber. And last but never least, the superhero folks we work with, Andrea Magyar and the team at Penguin, our photographer Ryan Szulc, prop stylist Madeleine Johari and food stylist Nancy Midwicki.

In special honor of Amber Daun Jones, January 1, 1993 – June 17, 2013. Much love to Craig, Sheila and Tana.

INDEX